Honouring
greatness of spirit
and
transformative leadership
in Asia

The Magsaysay Awards were constituted in memory of Ramon Del Fierro Magsaysay who was the President of the Philippines from 1953 to 1957. Magsaysay's principles and thoughts left an indelible impact not only on his own countrymen but also on the people of the entire world as he exemplified the highest form of leadership characterised by justice, equality and selfless service.

The Magsaysay Awards were first given in 1958 and continue till today. The Magsaysay Awards are bestowed on persons and organisations for their selfless leadership and whose lives and works have made Asia a better place to live in by addressing issues of human development across boundaries of culture, politics and religion with courage and creativity. The Awards are given in six categories: government service; public service; community leadership; journalism, literature and creative communication arts; peace and international understanding and the category, emergent leadership was added in the year 2000. A person working in any part of Asia is eligible for these awards regardless of caste, creed, religion or gender.

It is hoped that reading about the lives and works of the Indians who have been honoured with the Magsaysay Award will inspire young people to apply their talents and energies to selfless and innovative service, preserving the values of integrity, respect for human dignity and principled governance that characterised the work of the late President Ramon Magsaysay.

The Magsaysay Credo

I believe that government starts at the bottom and moves upward, for government exists for the welfare of the masses of the nation.

I believe that he who has less in life should have more in law.

I believe that the little man is fundamentally entitled to a little bit more food in his stomach, a little more cloth on his back and a little more roof over his head.

I believe that this nation is endowed with a vibrant and stout heart, and possesses untapped capabilities and incredible resiliency.

I believe that a high and unwavering sense of morality should pervade all spheres of government activity.

I believe that the pulse of government should be strong and steady, and the men at the helm imbued with missionary zeal.

I believe in the majesty of constitutional and legal processes, in the inviolability of human rights.

I believe that the free world is collectively strong, and that there is neither need nor reason to compromise the dignity of man.

I believe that communism is iniquity, as is the violence it does to the principles of Christianity.

I believe that the President should set the example of a big heart, an honest mind, sound instincts, the virtue of healthy impatience and an abiding love for the common man.

Pandurang Shastri Athavale 138
T.N. Seshan 141
Mahasweta Devi 149
Mahesh Chander Mehta 154
Jockin Arputham 161
Aruna Roy 167
Rajendra Singh 171
Sandeep Pandey 177
James Michael Lyngdoh 182
Shantha Sinha 186
Laxminarayan Ramdas 190
V. Shanta 194
Arvind Kejriwal 198
Palagummi Sainath 203
Prakash Amte and Mandakini Amte 208
Deep Joshi 213

Contents

Magsaysay Credo	7
Vinoba Bhave	9
C.D. Deshmukh	14
Amitabha Chowdhury	19
Mother Teresa	24
Verghese Kurien, Tribhuvandas K. Patel and Dara N. Khurody	29
Jayaprakash Narayan	34
Kamaladevi Chattopadhyay	39
Satyajit Ray	45
M.S. Swaminathan	50
M.S. Subbulakshmi	55
B.G. Verghese	59
Sombhu Mitra	63
Ela Ramesh Bhatt	69
R.S. Arole and M.R. Arole	73
Gour Kishore Ghosh	79
Pramod Karan Sethi	84
Chandi Prasad Bhatt	89
Manibhai Desai	94
Arun Shourie	99
R.K. Laxman	104
Murlidhar Devidas Amte	108
Lakshmi Chand Jain	113
K.V. Subbanna	118
Pandit Ravi Shankar	123
Banoo Jehangir Coyaji	127
Kiran Bedi	133

Established 1912
100 Years of
Excellence in Publishing

rajpal

₹ 325

ISBN : 9788170288589

GREATNESS OF SPIRIT

Edited by Meera Johri

Printed at Deepika Enterprises, Delhi

RAJPAL & SONS

1590, Madarsa Road, Kashmere Gate, Delhi-110006
Phone : 011-23869812, 23865483, 23867791
website : www.rajpalpublishing.com
e-mail : sales@rajpalpublishing.com
www.facebook.com/rajpalandsons

GREATNESS OF SPIRIT

Profiles of Indian Magsaysay Award Winners

Meera Johri

rajpal

VINOBA BHAVE

Awarded for Community Leadership (1958)

Famous for his bhoodan *(gift of land) and* sarvodaya *(welfare of community) movements in India, Vinoba Bhave became a leader of the masses encouraged by the teachings of the* Bhagwad Gita. *Deeply impressed with Mahatma Gandhi, he contributed his bit to the country's freedom struggle. His spirituality was connected to the society. Thus, despite his saintly disposition, he was influenced by the social environment which was witness to a turbulent political period. He appealed to the people to become self-reliant for fighting against social injustice and religious discord. It was because of his responsible contribution to social issues and as an advocate of non-violence and human rights that he was one of the first Magsaysay awardees in 1958.*

Vinoba Bhave, who launched two revolutionary movements -- the *bhoodan* (gift of land) and *sarvodaya* (welfare of the masses), said, "Do not allow yourself to imagine that revolutionary thinking can

be propagated by governmental power." He considered all revolutions as "spiritual at the source. All my activities have the sole purpose of achieving a union of hearts."

Vinoba Bhave, whose full name was Vinayak Narhari Bhave, was born on 11 September 1895 in a high-ranking Chitapavan Brahmin family in Gacoda village of Colaba district in Maharashtra. His mother Rukmini Devi was largely responsible for his spiritual growth. It was under her influence that Vinoba Bhave came to read about all the saints and philosophers of Maharashtra. He was particularly interested in Mathematics.

In 1916, Vinoba Bhave, while going to Bombay to appear for his intermediate examination, he changed his mind and took a detour to reach Benaras. This was because of an overpowering urge to acquire constructive knowledge and learn about the omnipotent God. At Benaras, he made an intensive study of the ancient Pauranic treatise in Sanskrit. In fact, it was this experience which gave a new direction to his life.

Once, on hearing Gandhiji speak at Benaras Hindu University, Vinoba Bhave got so impressed that he wrote a letter to the leader. After exchange of some correspondence, Gandhiji invited Vinoba Bhave to meet him at Kochrab Ashram in Ahmedabad. On 7 June 1916, Vinoba met Gandhiji and was so influenced by the leader's thinking that it changed the entire course of his life. He established an unbreakable bond with Gandhiji. At his *ashram*, Vinoba began to participate in various activities, like reading and writing, spinning of yarn on the *charkha* and serving the people.

In 1921, at Gandhiji's insistence, Vinoba Bhave took charge of running the Wardha Ashram. Two years later, in 1923, he started a monthly newsletter, *Maharashtra Dharma*, in which his essays on the *Upanishads* were published. Gradually his involvement increased in Gandhiji's creative activities, like *khadi* (handspun cotton cloth), *gram udhyog* (village craft), new education and sanitation, etc.

In 1932, he was sent to jail by the British colonial government because of his fight against the British rule. Within the prison walls, Vinoba Bhave daily gathered all his fellow prisoners to give them a series of lectures on the *Gita* in Marathi. Later on, his lectures were published in a compiled form under the title, *Gita Pravachane* (Talks on the *Gita*) which was later translated into all Indian languages. These lectures reached overseas and were translated into many foreign languages too. Vinoba Bhave said that his other contributions may be forgotten by the people but his lectures and his books would always be remembered.

In December 1932, he shifted to Nalwadi from where he experimented with his idea of supporting himself by spinning yarn alone. Later when he fell sick in 1938, he shifted to Paunar Ashram which remained his headquarters.

In 1940, he was initiated into the *satyagraha* movement by Mahatma Gandhi, who included him in the Quit India Movement two years later. When India attained Independence, Vinoba continued to read and write, his religious outlook widening in all directions and synthesising the truths of different religions. This is revealed by his hymn "*Om tat...*" which contains symbols of many religions. He practically renounced the world and began to lead the life of an ascetic. He felt that the average villager in India led a very deprived life and so tried to find a solution to the problem on the basis of a firm spiritual foundation. This formed the core of his *sarvodaya* and the *bhoodan* movement. As a part of the movement, Vinoba travelled on foot from village to village, pleading with the people to donate land so that it could be distributed among the landless to help them improve their lives. And how effective his movement proved!

In 1958, Vinoba Bhave was awarded the Magsaysay Award for his novel *bhoodan* and *sarvodaya* movement, organised for the welfare of the deprived common masses.

The strength of Vinoba Bhave's sincerity and leadership can also be gauged from the fact that he managed to persuade the dacoits of Chambal region to surrender themselves. So inspired were they by Vinoba, that of their own accord, they readily laid down their arms and surrendered.

In 1970, Vinoba Bhave announced his intention to stay only at Paunar where he observed a year's silence from 25 Decemeber 1974 to 25 December 1975. As a staunch supporter of Mahatma Gandhi, he was a non-controversial supporter of the Congress Party. But when the then Prime Minister Indira Gandhi imposed a state of Emergency in 1975, striking a severe blow to democracy and the Constitution, Vinoba Bhave continued to repose his faith in Mrs Indira Gandhi and the Congress. When she went to meet him, since he was observing a state of silence, he conveyed his message to her by writing on a slate, "Emergency is the need of the hour." He called it the *anushasan parva* (time for discipline). This dragged him into a controversy as his spiritual beliefs and social concern came to be looked upon with scepticism.

Vinoba Bhave was not only a freedom fighter and social reformer but also an educated writer and philosopher. He has written many books and translated numerous Sanskrit books to make them accessible to the common man. He was a linguist with an excellent command of Marathi, Hindi, English, Urdu and Sanskrit and was an active social reformer too. He made the message of *Gita* accessible to the common man through the many books that he wrote to convey its message. He wrote brief introductions to and criticisms of several religious and philosophical works like the *Vedanta*, works of Adi Shankaracharya, the Bible and the Quran. At the same time, many of his books on politics and his political views were published. In this respect his *Teesri Shakti* (Third Power) and *Swaraj Shastra* (Political Treatise) are particularly worth mentioning.

In November 1982, Vinoba fell seriously ill. He decided to give up his life and refused to take food, water or medicine. This

practice is very common in the Jain community who call this *sallekhana* or *praayopaveshan* (renocuncement of life by refusing food and water). On 15 November 1982, he died a peaceful death.

In the year 1983, Vinoba Bhave was posthumously awarded the Bharat Ratna, the highest civilian honour in India.

C.D. DESHMUKH

Awarded for Public Service (1959)

In 1918, Chintaman Dwarkanath Deshmukh stood first in the Indian Civil Services (ICS) examination and took up government employment. Before 1947, the examination was held only in London. After Independence, ICS was renamed as Indian Administrative Service (IAS) and its examination is now held at different centres all over India. He became the first Indian Governor of the Reserve Bank of India where he became well known as an independent-minded stabilising force. He later became the Union Finance Minister. He introduced basic reforms, instituted the salutary practice of giving annually a complete picture of the national economy and played a prominent role in international finance as India's delegate to a series of monetary conferences. He, along with Jose Vasquez Aguilar, was jointly awarded the Magsaysay Award for skilful, devoted and exemplary service to the government.

C.D. Deshmukh is essentially known for bringing about educational reforms and building the institutional machinery for providing agricultural credit to farmers.

He was born on 14 January 1896 at Nata, which is located next to the Raigarh fort in Maharashtra. His father, Dwarkanath Ganesh Deshmukh, was a respected lawyer and his mother, Bhagirathi Bai, a pious lady.

Deshmukh passed matriculation in 1912 from Bombay University in first division. He was awarded the Jagannath Shanker Sett Scholarship for Sanskrit. In 1917, he graduated from Cambridge University, London in the field of Natural Sciences Tripos with Botany, Chemistry and Geography as his subjects. At the same time he won the Frank Smart Prize in Botany. In 1918, he appeared for the Indian Civil Service examination held in London and stood first.

At that time, Deshmukh was only twenty-four years old. For most of the next twenty-one years, from 1918 to 1939, he worked on various posts in the government of Central Provinces and Berar. In this provincial government, he was probably the youngest among those who held the position of Revenue Secretary and Finance Secretary. While spending his holidays in London, he worked as one of the secretaries at the Second Round Table Conference in which Mahatma Gandhi participated. Mahatma Gandhi asked him to prepare the memorandum for the Cenral Provinces and Berar government. This note pertained to an enquiry to be conducted by Sir Otto Niemeyer and on the basis of which a policy on financial relations between the Centre and this province had to be finalised under the Government of India Act, 1935. This note was so comprehensively pepared that it won high acclaim for Deshmukh.

In July 1939, Deshmukh was appointed Liaison Officer for the Reserve Bank to keep the Government of India in touch with the affaris of the Reserve Bank. Three months later, he was

appointed Secretary of the Central Board of the Reserve Bank and two years later, in December 1941, he became the Deputy Governor. On 11 August 1943, he became the Governor and continued as such till 30 June 1949.

Deshmukh proved a very effective Governor as he made a remarkable contribution during his tenure by converting the Reserve Bank from a private shareholders' bank into a nationalised bank. He got an enactment passed for a comprehensive legislation to regulate the banking companies. As a result, long-term credit could be provided to industries by the Industrial Finance Corporation of India (IFCI). He also built up an institutional machinery to provide agricultural credit and for channellising Reserve Bank funds for development of agriculture. Under this scheme, the farmer could obtain loans for agricultural purposes. This wise move came in for plenty of appreciation as it was seen as an initiator of a major change from the conservative approach to a progressive one. Such an outlook was to prove beneficial in the long run.

In July 1944, Deshmukh participated in the Bretton Woods Conference where his constructive role made possible the establishment of International Monetary Fund (IMF) by the UN. At this time the International Bank for Reconstruction and Development (IBRD) was founded. In both these institutions, Deshmukh worked as a member on the Governors' Board for ten years and served as Chairman at the Joint Annual Meeting of these two institutions in 1950, at Paris.

In September 1949, the then Prime Minister, Jawahar Lal Nehru sent Deshmukh as Special Economic Ambassador to USA and Europe where he held constructive discussions with the USA on a programme for obtaining wheat loan. That very year, Nehru put forth a proposal for establishing the Planning Commission. When the Commission began its first proceedings on 1 April 1950, Deshmukh was appointed its member. Soon Deshmukh took charge as Finance Minister in Parliament, where he continued to work

till 1956. While occupying this ministerial post, substantial changes were seen in the country's economic schemes and his opinions had a substantial impact on the country's growth.

Deshmukh made a remarkable contribution to the country's First and Second Five-Year Plans and succeeded in maintaining strict financial control over expenditure of public funds while encouraging economic development. As a result, a new Companies Act was formulated. The Imperial Bank was nationalised and the concept of Life Insurance Company was visualised.

From 1956 to 1960, Deshmukh played a constructive role in different phases of public service. In the realm of education and social service, he served as Chairman of the University Grants Commission. He helped to lay a solid foundation for improvement in the standard of the university education. It was during his tenure that the Delhi University earned the reputation of being the best in the country for higher education.

Apart from financial and education sectors, Deshmukh was employed in various government departments. From 1945 to 1964, he continued as President of the Indian Statistical Institute and in 1965, he occupied the post of President of the Indian Institute of Economic Growth, New Delhi. From 1957 to 1960, he served as Honorary Chairman of National Book Trust, India and in 1959 established the India International Centre where he remained its Director for life. From 1959 to 1973, Deshmukh took the lead in appointing the Board of Governors for Administrative Staff College of India at Hyderabad. This way he handled the charge of many posts at the same time for many years as can be seen from the overlapping of dates.

Along with his wife Durgabai, Deshmukh participated in multifaceted social work, especially in the functional literacy and family planning work undertaken by the Andhra Mahila Sabha – a social organisation founded by Durgabai, his wife. He became its President after his wife's death.

A number of prestigious universities and institutions, international as well as national, conferred on him honorary doctorates.

After retirement from all his duties, Chintaman Deshmukh became busy with his family. Gardening was his favourite hobby and his deep attachment to Sanskrit language prompted him to get a compilation of his poems published.

On 2 October 1982, C.D. Deshmukh bid goodbye to this world at the age of eighty-seven.

AMITABHA CHOWDHURY

Awarded for Journalism, Literature and Creative Communication Arts (1961)

Armed with ethical values and honesty, Amitabha Chowdhury worked as a professional journalist. While working for the Bengali press, he followed the doctrine of keeping the interest of the public uppermost in his mind when reporting either on a politician or an officer. He forever abided by this resolve right from the time of working as an assistant editor of the daily Bengali newspaper, Jugantar *till the highest position that he reached in his profession. Not for a moment did his resolve waver as he continued to fulfil his duties as an investigative journalist, working like a faithful citizen devoted to the welfare of the public. Amitabha Chowdhury was awarded the Magsaysay Award in 1961 for his scrupulous and probing investigative reporting in protection of individual rights and community interests.*

Amitabha was in the vanguard of new journalism in the Bengali press and his bold reports revealed his crusading spirit to the

problems of his fellowmen. He once said, "For positive journalism, there is no half way, no role of a neutralist, no scope for timidity in the name of so-called objectivity and no reason to indulge in nameless generalisaiton."

Born on 11 November 1927 at Calcutta, he does not even remember his father, Shishir Chowdhury, who died when Amitabha was only four-months old. His mother Preetirani Chowdhury brought him up.

Amitabha Chowdhury began his education at Chandranath High School in Calcutta. In 1944, he completed his matriculation from Dutta High School of Netrakona at Mymensing in East Bengal (present-day Bangladesh).

After matriculation, Amitabha studied in succession at A.M. College, St. Xavier's College and Ashutosh College to graduate in English (Honours), with Economics and Mathematics respectively as his subsidiary subjects.

As soon as he left college, Amitabha secured a job as a reporter in the esteemed daily, *Jugantar* of Bengal. *Jugantar* was a daily newspaper published by Calcutta's famous publishing house, *Amrita Bazaar Patrika* whose print run at the time was 72,00 copies per day. In 1952, while working with the *Jugantar*, Amitabha Chowdhury acquired his post-graduation degree from Calcutta University with modern Indian languages as his subject of specialisation.

During his journalistic career he depicted many vivid stories with insight and compassion on the human tragedy of mass migraton of refugees following the Partititon of India. He set a pattern for a new reportorial style in the Bengali press. He presented his views fearlessly and his humane style of writing came to be highly appreciated by the Bengali press and readers alike.

Later, given charge of parliamentary reporting after a period as an art critic, his simple and popular presentation of complicated legislative matters was also followed by his colleagues and it is now a common feature of modern Bengali journalism.

In 1956, Amitabha was appointed Assistant Editor of *Jugantar*. He was the youngest to hold this position on any major newspaper in Calcutta. His major contribution to Indian journalism was his exemplary weekly column titled 'Nepathya Darshan' (Scenes behind the Curtain). As is apparent from the title, he used it to highlight the scene not visible to the eyes. He voiced the legitimate grievances of the disgruntled Bengali intellectuals and the poor alike. As his byline, he used the name Sri Nirapeksha (Mr Impartial) to clarify that he was not a supporter of any particular group. Through this column, Amitabha wrote one thrilling story after another and this started a trend in investigative journalism. The column prompted Amitabha to place a proposal before the management of *Jugantar* saying that he would not claim any extra honorarium provided he was given a free hand to write on the subject of his choice. The management not only accepted his conditions but also gave him unfailing support through the many attacks and court actions it engendered. Free to write on subjects of his choice and to discontinue the column if it seemed advisable, he customarily researched each item meticuloulsly over a period of several months, wrote only about cases he could prove with irrefutable evidence and carefully checked the final proofs for the smallest typographical errors. Thus able to meet any lawsuit with equanimity, he earned for his newspaper and himself increasing respect and readership.

The impact of Amitabha Chowdhury's column can be gauged from the fact that during a full-scale parliamentary debate on his article regarding riots between the minority Bengalis and the majority Assamese in Assam, his article was translated into various languages because of its significance and distributed in Parliament in 1956. Performing as a one-man inquiry commission into the underlying causes and reasons for the administrations's failure to quell the outbreaks, his column became for the terrorised two million who comprised the Bengali-speaking minority of Assam their advocate.

Similarly in 1957, Amitabha's report on mismanagement in

the Damodar Valley Corporation prompted a parliamentary discussion and the Prime Minister ordered an enquiry to be conducted on its basis. The truth behind the questions raised by Amitabha in the enquiry report was duly revealed. As a result, not only was the statute amended, even the Chairman was asked to retire and a new Board for the project was constituted.

The plight of the common man was at the centre of his writings. Once, a fireman of a locomotive died as a result of the intense heat inside the locomotive, his wife and child were not entitled to any compensation because he had not been made permanent in his job despite working for four years. Amitabha's incisive and realistic presentation of the report forced the Railways to not only pay compensation to the victim's wife and child but also provide employment to his wife in the Railway Department.

There was this case of an Excise Inspector who lost his life while raiding an illicit brewery. The readership of *Jugantar* responded with contributions. The Inspector's case caught the attention of the State Legislature through Amitabha's column written under the pen name 'Mr Impartial' which made the management pay compensation. Amitabha Chowdhury's elaborate research into the service career and savings of the Excise Inspector showed him to be a notably honest and brave employee and a pension was assured for his widow as well as an education allowance for his children.

During his tenure, Amitabha raised more than 250 cases of abuse of power through which corruption and nepotism in the high-level machinery of the government came to light and accordingly the concerned officials were duly punished.

Along with this, Amitabha's column created an environment of debate on many issues of public welfare and helped to solve successfully many social issues. Innumerable examples can be cited to prove Amitabha Chowdhury's role in bringing justice to the aggrieved party and in public welfare. He countered the belief

that the journalist when reporting a news item should always remain indifferent. His belief was that the journalist had to become a supporter of one or the other aggrieved party to take up the fight on that party's behalf. He said that a true journalist always stood in favour of truth by becoming its strength. But it was also essential that while trying to reach the root of the truth, the journalist should remain impartial and desist from harbouring any preconceived notion. But he clarified, "It is the duty of a journalist to take sides between good and evil, between the sufferer and the one inflicting the suffering."

Amitabha Chowdhury also got the opportunity to participate in a seminar organised by the American Press Institute in 1958. In 1959 he got married to Neepa, a well-known artiste of the time.

He was invited to participate as a trainer in two Asian seminars organised by the International Press Institute. The seminars were organised in Delhi in November 1960 and at Lahore in March 1961 respectively. In these seminars, the articles written by Amitabha Chowdhury in his investigative column were read out and discussions held on them. Among the participants from India and Pakistan, many adopted his style of presenting the facts. He displayed his journalistic skill and uncompromising integrity by upholding high ethical standards in his profession as a guardian of the public conscience.

MOTHER TERESA

Awarded for Peace and International Understanding (1962)

It was indeed a matter of immense pride for India to have Mother Teresa, the daughter of Albanian parents of Yugoslavia, as its citizen. In 1948, when Mother Teresa visited India, she was deeply moved at the rampant poverty and the plight of the poor who were either homeless or living in slums. With the permission of Pope II, Mother Teresa founded a new Indian congregation, the Missionaries of Charity, an organisation fully devoted to the service of the poor. She obtained Indian citizenship by joining this organisation and involving herself in this project. Along with the physically challenged and underprivileged persons, it was the lepers who became the centre of her attention. The lepers were looked down upon with revulsion by the society. The way she devoted herself to this selfless service and built her organisation showed the path of voluntary service to the world. She was awarded the Ramon Magsaysay Award of 1962 for peace and international understanding in recognition of her merciful

Desai was one of the many who promised Mahatma Gandhi "to lay my ashes in Uruli-Kanchan" for rural development work.

Manibhai Bhimbhai Desai was born on 27 April 1920 at Kosmada village of Surat district in Gujarat. His father, Bhimbhai Faqirbhai Desai, was a distinguished farmer among the adjoining ten to fifteen villages. Manibhai had four brothers and one sister, each of whom had been inculcated with a "very strong common sense" by their mother, Ramibahen Desai.

Manibhai began his education in 1927 at the village school. That very year his father died and his mother took over the entire responsibility to bring up her children. Manibhai was a student who invariably topped his class and his contribution in sports and scout was also praiseworthy.

Simplicity was inborn in Manibhai since childhood. His mother used to worry about her son getting spoilt and to avoid this being so, she sent him to her cousin to study in Surat. Her sister had her own five to six children and the family was far from well-off. In such a situation, Manibhai had to attend to many household chores. His mother had given him a cow so that he would never face any shortage of milk. Manibhai tended to the cow and attended to all other duties with full devotion. Not once did he complain against it, but his mother did not like it. It so happened that one day, she suddenly decided to visit her son and to her shock found Manibhai cleaning the glass of the kerosene lanterns. She took him away and put him in a hostel. Next year, he was enrolled in Anavil Ashram from where he passed his high school in 1939. The foundation for self-reliance was laid here in Manibhai.

After high school, Manibhai Desai joined the M.T.B. Sarvajanik College in Surat. This institute was attached to Bombay University. Manibhai's elder brother wanted him to become an engineer and so made him study physics and mathematics. In 1942, Manibhai obtained a degree in Junior Bachelor of Science and entered the final year of college. At that time Gandhiji's freedom movement

was at its peak. On 9 August 1942, the British Government imprisoned all the Congress leaders. Manibhai, without taking permission from his family, left his college and jumped into Gandhiji's freedom movement.

He renounced all his property, chose celibacy and committed himself to serving the rural poor. He participated in Gandhi's Salt Movement and distributed the illegally prepared salt in his village.

In 1943, Manibhai, along with Gandhiji, was put in prison where he discussed with Gandhiji the need for village development. In 1944, after getting released from prison, he decided to give up all his plans of becoming an engineer. He instead chose to work for development of the villages. In April 1943, Manibhai appeared for the examination of his last paper and that very evening caught the train going to Gandhiji's *ashram*.

At the *ashram*, he had a memorable meeting with Gandhiji and his reference to it is no less interesting. Gandhiji said to Manibhai, "First of all, you must visit the villages and forget all that you have studied."

Manibhai, a first-class degree holder in physics and mathematics, was shocked at this. He asked, "Bapu, are you against education?"

Bapu replied, "I did not tell you this because I am against your being educated. I want you to rid yourself of all the sophistication which a college and society impart to make you educated…"

With this first lesson learnt, Desai reached his village. He began to gather the villagers of Kosmada into a group. After about four months, Desai received a letter from Gandhiji saying, "Come and meet me immediately at Sevagram."

The fact that Desai was to leave the village shocked the villagers. They had come to rely upon him and his work. Even his family was taken aback because he had not mentioned anything about his meeting with Gandhi to them. Anyway, he left after

convincing the villagers that since Gandhiji had sent for him, it should be a matter of pride for their village.

On 18 April 1945, Manibhai Desai met Gandhji at Sevagram Ashram in Wardha. Gandhiji wanted to establish a centre for the poor to treat patients at the minimum of expenses through nature cure. Before taking action, Gandhiji wanted to test Manibhai. He entrusted the duty of cleaning the latrines to Manibhai and also gave him the responsibility of learning to prepare manure from waste products and excreta. Desai did this work dutifully for one-and-a-half months. Satisfied with his devotion and discipline, Gandhiji invited him to join him as a member of his personal staff and entrusted him the task of keeping accounts.

On Gandhiji's instructions, Desai began to work in the dairy *ashram* at Uruli-Kanchan. This *ashram* became a centre for important activities and for nature cure for the poor villagers. In another programme of this centre, a school with thirty boys was established in a farmhouse so that they could develop into modern farmers in future. In villages, Desai helped in setting up cooperatives which would provide loans to farmers without going through the moneylender. On 90 acres of land he set up a pasture and a cooperative farming society to allow the landless farmers to earn their livelihood throughout the year.

In 1967, Desai started the Bhartiya Agro Industries Foundation (BAIF) in which Gandhiji's doctrine of cow protection was put to action. In 1950, Desai personally performed surgery on dead cows by training himself to become a veterinary doctor. Manibhai, through artificial insemination of cows from Denmark and Britain, prepared a new breed which could yield more milk. Similarly, to protect animals from the foot-and-mouth disease, a vaccine was prepared here through which hundreds of animals could be saved every year. With other facilities and latest modes of treatment provided at the Indian Agro Industries Foundation, the country's economy began to show improvement.

In 1982, Manibhai Desai wrote in the *BAIF Newsletter*: "At BAIF we have never ever looked down on the rural people as either pitiable or contemptible creatures. India's rural people represent perhaps the finest specimen of hardy manhood."

After spending seventy-three years of industrious life, Manibhai Bhimbhai Desai breathed his last in 1993.

ARUN SHOURIE

Awarded for Journalism, Literature and Creative Communication Arts (1982)

The effort to bring to light the state of society through journalism, art and literature demands immense bravery and fearlessness because it entails attacks on the administration or the government, leading to some kind of loss or a problem. But people engaged in such work are prepared to face the consequences. Arun Shourie too belongs to this category. He regularly raises his voice against corruption, discord and injustice in the society while speaking in favour of justice. For this he has had to suffer immensely but his desire for truth always prevails. In 1982 he was awarded the Magsaysay Award for his constructive journalism for employing his pen as an effective adversary of corruption, inequality and injustice.

In human history abuse of power has been an irresistible temptation. Speaking for the abused and upholding justice becomes the task

of those who care and have the courage. Arun Shourie is one such brave soul.

Arun Shourie was born at Jalandhar (Punjab) on 2 November 1941. His father, Hari Dev Shourie, was an eminent government official. Arun is the first child of his father. He has a sister Nalini and a brother Deepak.

Arun had his schooling at Modern School in New Delhi. He then took admission in St. Stephen's College of Delhi University and in 1961 obtained his Honours degree in Economics. After he had completed his first year of MA in Economics from the same college, he ran into the Dean of Maxwell School of Public Administration of Syracuse University, New York. The Dean offered him a full fellowship for studying at his institute. Arun Shourie completed his M.A. in Economics at the institute in New York and in 1966 obtained a doctorate in Economics.

That very year, Arun Shourie appeared for an interview under the 'Young Professionals Programme' of World Bank and returned to India. Here he began his career by working for the Tata Group of Industries. Within three months he received the news of his appointment in World Bank at Washington. Before leaving for USA, he got married to Anita Shukla on 12 February 1967 and left for Washington along with his wife. His tenure at World Bank was of five years duration. But on settling down to a routine, he began to feel restless "maybe because of the distance, because of reading, emotional attachment to the family, to friends, I really don't know," as he said. He therefore applied for a Homi Bhabha Fellowship.

For 1972 to 1974 Arun Shourie received this fellowship besides getting appointed as Consultant in the Planning Commission of India. The fellowship gave him complete freedom to pursue his interests and remain at his post at the Planning Commission. Here he got a ringside view of developments in politics and administration. Many issues related to violation of human rights and the

Constitution aroused journalistic curiosity within him and he wrote his first political article, titled 'On Keeping Silent', which was published in 1975. In this article he had predicted the imposition of the state of Emergency.

On completion of his fellowship, in 1974, Arun Shourie returned to the World Bank and joined the Policy Planning and Programme Review Department. The department was under the control of Mahbub-ul-Haq of Pakistan and whom Arun Shourie held in high regard.

At this juncture Arun Shourie suddenly received a message from Dr J.P. Naik, Director of Indian Council of Social Science Research (ICSSR), asking him to return to India and present his dissertation on some abstract topic and "then do what you want". Arun Shourie chose the topic, 'Mahatma Gandhi's Philosophy and the Tradition of Indian Movement and Current Situation'.

Between March 1977 and 1978, Arun Shourie studied the ancient Hindu treatise on *dharma* and was drawn to Jayaprakash Narayan's movement. During this period he wrote political articles whose themes were political power, corruption, disregard for democracy, etc. These articles were published in *Seminar*, *Mainstream*, *India Today*, *Deccan Herald* and the *Indian Express*. In 1978 these were further reprinted. Further, three to four other essays by Arun Shourie were also published and these had already been printed in *Systems of Fascism* and *Washington Essays*.

In 1978, when the Janata Party came to power, Arun Shourie was selected to work for the Press Commission of India. He was appointed to write on the condition of the Indian press. He worked here till August 1978 and submitted his manuscript on *Hinduism* for publication. On 1 January 1979, Arun Shourie was appointed Executive Editor of the *Indian Express*.

In *Indian Express*, Shourie's journalism was based on criticism of the establishment since the very beginning. In 1981, he exposed Abdul Rehman Antulay, Chief Minister of Maharashtra, for his

involvement in a scam. In his articles, Shourie revealed that Antulay had deposited in his personal trust lakhs of dollars earned illegally through various government schemes. The trust was being run in Indira Gandhi's name. On exposure of the scam, Chief Minister Antulay was forced to submit his resignation. This was the first time that based on a newspaper report, the government was forced to remove a very important and high-ranking personality.

As a result of this step by Arun Shourie, the Bombay office of *Indian Express* faced many labour problems. Antulay had incited the labour to go on strike and demand double wages from the new Workers' Union. With this, the government imposed repressive measures on *Indian Express* and cases were filed by different organisations against the newspaper. In 1982, the proprietor, Ramnath Goenka, sacked Arun Shourie under government pressure.

Form 1982 to 1986, Arun Shourie wrote many articles as a freelancer for many newpapars and journals. At the same time, he became the General Secretary of the People's Union of Civil Liberties. In 1986, *The Times of India* appointed him as its Executive Editor but here too he did not stay long as in 1987, Ramnath Goenka recalled him back to *Indian Express.* During this period, Arun Shourie raised the controversial Bofors issue against Rajiv Gandhi for having taken a cut in the purchase of the Bofors gun. In his argument, Arun Shourie was supported by the entire press along with the *Indian Express* management. At that time, Rajiv Gandhi was the Prime Minister of India. Meanwhile the Indian Government filed 300 cases against the *Indian Express.* Even the loans given by various banks to the newspaper were stopped. But Arun Shourie continued with his campaign. In 1990, due to his disagreement with the *Indian Express's* editorial policy, Arun Shourie resigned. Here his disagreement was over the introduction of the reservation policy as per the Mandal Commission report which the then Prime Minister, Vishwanath Pratap Singh, had approved. On leaving the *Indian Express,* Arun Shourie began to devote his time to writing

for different newspapers, journals and books which were published in the country. In 1990, he was awarded the title 'Journalist of the Year' and honoured with the Padma Bhushan Award too. In 1999, Arun Shourie became a member of the the Rajya Sabha.

He is a member of the Bharatiya Janata Party (BJP) and has also served as Minister of Disinvestment, Communication and Information Technology in the Government of Indian under Atal Bihari Vajpayee's prime ministership during 1999-2004. As Disinvestment Minister, he led the sale of Maruti, VSNL, Hindustan Zinc, among other. His position as Minister was a controversial one, but he and his secretary Pradip Baijal are much respected for kick-starting what people believe was a best-in-class process. In a poll of India's top 100 CEOs in February 2004, he was ranked the most outstanding minister of Mr. Vajpayee's government.

In the year 2000, Shourie pledged the entire amount (Rs. 11.90 crore) or discretionary spending available to him under Members of Parliament Local Area Development Scheme (MPLADS) to setting up of Bio-Sciences and Bio-engineering Department at the Indian Institute of Technology, Kanpur. In 2005, he displayed his commitment to the cause by again pledging Rs. 11 crore for developing a separate and well-equipped building for Environmental Sciences and Environmental Engineering at the institute.

R.K. LAXMAN

Awarded for Journalism, Literature and Creative Communication Arts (1984)

In the field of journalism, cartoonists are considered an unusual breed of people. By drawing a few lines they can highlight or reduce to dust anybody's character in the society. Their style of expression can deliver a strong blow to the subject of caricature. R.K. Laxman too had been a cartoonist endowed with the capacity to draw attractive cartoons. With a deep understanding of political and social realities, he was able to see through many things and express the reality through his protagonist — the Common Man with a closed umbrella. Laxman received the 1984 Ramon Magsaysay Award for his incisive, witty, never malicious cartoons illuminating India's political and social issues.

Cartoonists are a rare breed within the journalistic fraternity, who can pierce the heart of any problem with a few lines of a sketch. What is more their message can be understood equally well by both the less literate and the erudite. R.K. Laxman was one such

gifted cartoonist who could blacken the prospects of a public personality with a single sketch of his chin or nose.

Rasipuram Krishnaswamy Iyer Laxman, popularly known as R.K. Laxman was born on 23 October 1924 in Mysore. He took birth in a Tamil family and was the youngest son amongst five others. His father was a headmaster in school.

Laxman was famous for his drawings even at school. He used to draw pictures anywhere at all – on the walls of his home, on the door, or here and there. His teacher appreciated his drawings. Among his drawings were cartoons of his teachers. Once Laxman drew a *peepal* tree and it was greatly appreciated by those around him.

Laxman was deeply influenced by a British cartoonist, Sir David Low. Laxman used to talk frequently about him and for long considered his name to be Cow because he misread it due to the latter's stylistic signature. This he has even mentioned in his autobiography, *The Tunnel of Time.*

It was in his nature to draw all the time since childhood. All kinds of drawings would find place in his collection of drawings and he even wrote in his autobiogray, "I drew objects that caught my eye outside the window of my room – the dry twigs, leaves and lizard-lilke creatures crawling about, the servant chopping firewood and, of course, a number of crows in various postures on the rooftops of the buildings opposite."

Laxman's idyllic childhood was shaken for a while when his father suffered a paralytic stroke and died a year later. It shocked him but the elders at home bore the increased responsibility, while Laxman continued with his schooling. In school itself Laxman had decided to take up art and painting. He submitted his application for admission to JJ School of Arts in Bombay. Laxman received the reply from the Dean saying that his drawings lacked "the kind of talent to qualify for enrolment in our institution as a student" and refused him admission. Laxman took admission in B.A. at Mysore University. Alongside, he continued sending his cartoons

for publication in *Swarajya,* while working as a freelance artist. His drawings of the mythological character Narad began to appear in animated films.

Laxman's initial drawings appeared not only in *Swarajya* but *Blitz* also . When studying at Maharaja College in Mysore, he had illustrated stories for his elder brother, R.K. Narayan, and these were published in the *Hindu.* Meantime Laxman began to draw cartoons on the political scene and these were published in the local newspapers and in *Swatantra.* He also drew cartoons for the Kannada comic journal, *Koravanji*, which was founded in 1942 by Dr M. Shivaram. He encouraged Laxman considerably with his cartoons. During his summer holidays, Laxman worked for the Gemini Studios in Madras.

Laxman's first regular job was with the *Free Press Journal*, where he was taken as a political cartoonist. He then joined *The Times of India* where he continued to work for more than fifty years.

In *The Times of India*, a feature cartoon under the title 'You Said It' was published in which a Common Man with typical features made a sharp and true comment on the Indian life. This publication began in 1961. Apart from *The Times of India*, these cartoons were pubished in the form of an inexpensive paperback edition. Amongst the other books published, in an introduction to one book, it was thus written about Laxman's work: "The cartoonist works for such an industry where the value of time is significant. It is like a sword hanging over his head till the drawing has been completed and sent. Each cartoon, one after another, encouraged a still better piece — shortage of tomatoes, an imminent danger of attack, Five-Year Plans, pot-holes on roads, corruption, meteorological predictions, space journey to the moon — the subject could be anything."

No matter what the theme was, the caricature of the common man remained the same — his nose, eyebrows, hair sprouting from the ears and peeping out from below the bald pate, his moustache,

his coat — nothing changed, bu every time the same protagonist was presented in a new style, with a new impact. For the readers, the Common Man became a signature of Laxman's art.

Apart from *The Times of India*, Laxman drew pictures for many books. In the very popular stories *Malgudi Days* by his elder brother, R.K. Narayan, the pictures were drawn by Laxman. The book without the cartoons by Laxman would have appeared incomplete. Gattu, the mascot of Asian Paints, is a creation of Laxman's art. His cartoons were used in the Hindi film *'Mr & Mrs 55'* also.

Besides cartoons and illustrations, he wrote some novels too, among which his autobiographical *A Tunnel to Time* is included. Description of R.K. Laxman's nature and his ability to capture humour can be summarised thus:

Once an American cartoonist Ranan Lurie asked Laxman, "Who is the best cartoonist in India?"

Laxman replied, "I."

When he was asked, "After you, who is second?", his reply was the same, "I."

On being asked for further names, his reply was, "I."

This type of simplicity is reflected in one of his cartoons too. There is a statue of Pandit Nehru and below it stands Laxman's Common Man along with Nehru himself. The Common Man is saying to Pandit Nehru, "...I don't know who this man is...but every time I vote for him..."

R.K. Laxman was decorated with many awards and honours. He was awarded the Padma Bhushan and Padma Vibhushan by the Government of India. The *Hindustan Times* presented him the Durga Ratna Gold Medal and the *Indian Express* gave him the B.D. Goenka Award.

R.K. Laxman divides his time between Bombay and Poona with his wife. While Laxman is a cartoonist, his wife Kamala is a writer.

MURLIDHAR DEVIDAS AMTE

Awarded for Public Service (1985)

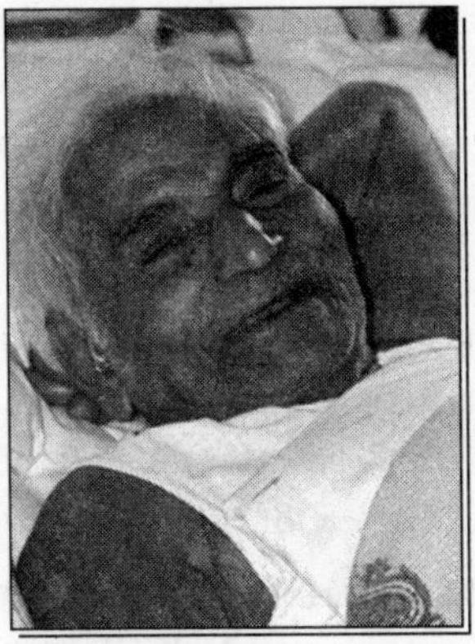

According to Indian tradition, giving alms and donations to the needy and helpless out of sympathy is considered sacred, but Baba Devidas Murlidhar Amte rejected this tradition to present his new philosophy of life. He said, "Do not give alms to the poor; do some work for them; provide them with opportunities and facilities so that they can lead a life of self-respect by doing something constructive in society." Baba Amte, on seeing the plight of lepers, resolved to do some constructive work for their welfare as they were boycotted by the society. And to work towards this goal, he renounced his personal wealth, facilities, everything and began to work for rehabilitation, welfare and relief for the lepers. For his work-oriented rehabilitation of Indian leprosy patients and other handicapped outcasts, Baba Amte was awarded the Magsaysay Award of 1985.

Charity is our traditional response to the disabled, but Murlidhar Devidas Amte believed in the philosophy that "charity destroys,

work builds" and accordingly he gave thousands of social outcasts the chance to prosper and become productive members of the local economy.

Murlidhar Devidas Amte was born on 26 December 1914 at Hingandhar village of Wardha district in Maharashtra. His parents Devidas Amte and Laxmibai Marpakwar were rich Brahmin landlords. He was called Baba, a nickname given by his parents out of affection. Amte was of rebellious nature since his childhood. He used to insist on eating and drinking with untouchables. While his parents wanted him to concentrate on his studies, he preferred playing with the servants' children. This led to a strained relationship between the father and the son.

Baba Amte studied law to become a barrister and ran a lucrative practice at Wardha. He also acquired large wealth as a legacy from his family.

In that era, leprosy was considered a God's curse and lepers were treated as outcasts by society. They were not only deprived of family life, welfare and health, but also looked down upon by society. As a result, their condition was pitiable and no one had any sympathy for them.

In such a scenario, Baba Amte not only left his flourishing law profession, his inherited wealth and all kinds of comfort, but also vowed to work for the welfare of lepers and devote his life for alleviation of leprosy.

He got married when working as a lawyer. But only a few weeks after his marriage, he discussed things out with his wife and left his profession and home to begin working among lepers.

A very memorable incident took place in his life. Once he saw a leper die slowly in an advanced stage of the disease and this disturbed him deeply. In 1951, he took admission in Calcutta's School of Tropical Medicines to acquire knowledge on leprosy. The very same year, he left home, taking along with him six lepers, one lame cow, his wife and family. He found 20 hectares of isolated,

rocky and barren land near Chandrapur in Maharashtra. On reaching near, he found the area infested with all kinds of animals, ranging from scorpions and snakes to leopards. Baba Amte established his Anandvan Ashram (Forest of Bliss) here and soon converted the area into an 'abode of happiness'.

Conversion of a forest area into an *ashram* had consumed a large portion of Baba Amte's time and money. In this respect he recalled an incident. A well had to be dug in an area of that rocky land. It took three weeks to reach 10 metres deep. He said, "Tears began to roll down our eyes because despite digging that far, the land was as dry as ever." Baba Amte did not lose hope, however, and kept encouraging others to continue digging. Ultimately, success was achieved to the extent that within two years the very same rocky land became rich enough to make them self-reliant in foodgrains and vegetables. With this, not only did Anandvan flourish, but also feelings of self-respect and self-reliance developed among its inhabitants.

After Anandvan, in 1957, Baba Amte built Ashokvan on an area of land measuring 40 hectares, north of Nagpur. After about a decade, he did the same at Somnath. As at Anandvan, arrangements were made for rehabilitation of the physically challenged and the lepers.

The tough life at Anandvan Ashram was not new to Baba Amte. He had served as a freedom fighter and was a staunch devotee of Mahatma Gandhi. He even spent some time at Gandhiji's *ashram.* He was no less impressed by Vinoba Bhave. Rabindranath Tagore's literature and work had also been responsible in moulding his personality.

While staying at the *ashram*, Baba Amte got deeply engrossed in taking care of the lepers who had accompanied him. He created an atmosphere at the *ashram* where the lepers could lead a life of self-respect while contributing their mite to the activities at the *ashram.* What could be described as the high point of Baba

Amte's sacrifice was when during the period of treatment and experimentation of drugs for fighting leprosy, he allowed leprosy germs to grow on his body so that the new drug for leprosy and the treatment regimen could first be tested on himself.

In 1974, Baba Amte established a people's brotherhood organisation for the welfare of the Madia Gond Adivasis. During his travels and tours of the country, Baba Amte met a boy whose innocence deeply influenced him. Baba was, however, shocked to learn that the Adivasis had never seen a wheel, never heard of India and in spite of the growth of civilisation elsewhere, they were suffering from injustice and neglect. Disturbed at the pitiable condition of the Adivasis, Baba Amte took up another responsibility and after calling over his newly married younger son and daughter-in-law, he entrusted to them the responsibility of the people's brotherhood campaign, though remaining involved with its acivities. His son and daughter-in-law ae also qualified doctors.

Besides taking care of the lepers at Anandvan, Baba Amte did work which revealed his consciousness and leadership qualities. In 1985, he launched a movement *'Bharat Jodo'* ('Integrate India') for maintaining the integrity of the country right from Kashmir in the north to Kanyakumari in the south. In this movement, the message of peace and protection of environment was conveyed.

In 1988, he launched another '*Bharat Jodo*' movement. This time his area of activity was to cover Gujarat in the west to Arunachal Pradesh in the east. In 1990, he left his *ashram* to set up his camp on the banks of River Narmada. Here he saw that injustice had been meted out to the local inhabitants by ignoring their rights to land. Construction of the Sardar Sarovar Dam was a source of danger for the local inhabitants living on its bank. Baba Amte, leaving the responsibility of the *ashram* on other inmates, directly reached the site to participate in the *'Narmada Bachao Andolan'* ('Save the Narmada' movement).

Baba Amte was decorated with many national and international

awards and honours. The Indian Government awarded him the Padma Shri in 1971 and the Padma Vibhushan in 1980. In 1983, he was awarded the Demin Dutton award. In 1988, Baba Amte received the G.D. Birla International Award and the UN Human Rights Award. The Templeton Prize by London, United Kingdom was awarded to him in 1990. That very year he was given the International Giraffe Award by America. Sweden Parliament awarded the Right Livelihood Award to him in 1992. In 1999, he was presented the International Gandhi Peace Prize and also India's Dr Ambedkar International Award.

Baba Amte had not been keeping well for several years in his later life. He was compelled to lie down on bed for much of the time due to severe spondylitis. He could walk but not sit erect and had to travel in a prone position. But he continued to build and plan. In 2007, he was diagnosed with leukaemia.

On 9 February 2008, Baba Murlidhar Devidas Amte took leave from this world at the age of 94 years. As per his last wish, he was buried and not cremated.

LAKSHMI CHAND JAIN

Awarded for Public Service (1989)

Governments of most developing nations are engaged in building the road to progress for their different communities living together with their many languages and cultures. It is often seen that advantages of economic growth, without filtering down to the poor and the needy, reach only those who are officials and are already well-off. Realising this shortcoming of the system, Lakshmi Chand Jain put forth the view that instead of having a completely machine-based economy, a labour-intensive economy would be ideal for the benefit of the poor and the needy. He suggested that democratic, voluntary groups and self-help units in villages could produce better results.Thus, on the basis of this principle, he got down to helping the proletariat. For his informed and selfless commitment to attack India's poverty at the grass-roots level, Lakshmi Chand Jain was awarded the Magsaysay Award of 1989.

On observing that benefits of economic growth and development often bypass the needy and reach the affluent, Lakshmi Chand Jain drew the conclusion that socio-economic problems can best be solved through village associations and voluntary agencies rather than the state machinery.

Lakshmi Chand Jain was born in Delhi on 13 December 1925. He was the eldest among his father's four children. Both his father, Phool Chand Jain, and mother, Chameli Devi, were freedom fighters and through them, Lakshmi Chand Jain inculcated the spirit of patriotism and service.

Some incidents regarding the development of his patriotic feelings are interesting. Once, early in the morning of a cold day in winter, Lakshmi Chand's father took him to a public meeting of Gandhiji. On seeing them, Gandhiji scolded his father for bringing a small child along in such a cold weather. Gandhiji took out his shawl and wrapped the young Lakshmi Chand in it, besides offering him dry fruits to eat. On another occasion, Lakshmi Chand was taken to hear Pandit Nehru's speech but being a child, he got lost in the crowd. Pandit Nehru searched him out and picking him up in his arms, handed him over to his grateful father.

Lakshmi Chand's education began in 1929. He studied in Delhi at the primary and secondary schools established by the Jains. He was a bright student and was appointed the headboy of his class. In 1939, he entered Hindu College of Delhi University. Initially he began studying science subjects to prepare for medical examination but after two years, he took up History and Philosophy as his subjects. He had a deep understanding of practical economics and this he applied regularly to life. In 1955, he attended a summer training programme in Economics organised by Harvard University. He even acquired non-formal education through his Oxford-educated wife, Devaki.

Lakshmi Chand's university education got disrupted midway due to many reasons. One of the prime reasons was the onset

of the Second World War. The Indian leaders demanded freedom first from the British Government before helping the British in the war, but the British Government did not accede to the demand. Gandhiji decided to exert pressure on the British by launching the 'Quit India' movement in August 1942. Lakshmi Chand Jain's father was imprisoned along with other Congress leaders. Lakshmi Chand along with other nationalist students jumped into the foray and began to work underground under the pseudonym Santosh. His revolutionary activities included snapping of telephone wires and making indigenous bombs, apart from writing, publishing and distributing literature of volatile nature. He also used to work as a messenger from one underground base to another.

In the midst of these activities, Lakshmi Chand Jain and his compatriots began to discuss the shape of the society to come once the British left India. For this purpose, they constituted a group called *'Parivartankaris'* ('Change Initiators'). Though influenced by Marxism, they were aware of the advantages and limitations of Marxism. They were also supporters of Gandhism.

After the Second World War got over, Lakshmi Chand completed his graduation and obtained a Masters degree in history. That very year he was appointed Vice Chairman of the students' branch of the Delhi Congress Party. Meanwhile the Asian Relations Conference held its meeting in India where Lakshmi Chand Jain played a key role in supervising the arrangements. Here he got the opportunity to meet many reputed leaders.

Soon after Independence, before Lakshmi Chand could get involved in any purposeful activity, the tragedy of Partition occurred and he got engrossed in overseeing the refugee camp at Hudson Lines as the Chief Supervisor. However, plans for the future of the country remained uppermost in his mind. He worked underground but before undertaking any activity, he used to ask himself, "Had Gandhiji been here, what would have he done?" By way of reply, whatever seemed appropriate to him, he would

begin doing that. Meanwhile he appointed civil engineers at a handsome salary for rehabilitation work while he himself got busy with the task of providing employment and training to displaced persons.

During the last days of 1947, Lakshmi Chand Jain met Kamaladevi Chattopadhyay. Both were shocked at a question posed by one of the refugees, who had asked, "What is our future…?"

At that moment Lakshmi Chand Jain regretted that such a question had never cropped up in his mind. Promptly he and Kamaladevi got down to discussions on how to find a way out for the refugees so that they could emerge from their camps and lead a normal life outside.

In 1948, Lakshmi Chand Jain, in cooperation with Kamaladevi Chattopadhyay, established the Indian Coopeative Union. This organisation took some of the refugees to a vacant plot some distance away from Delhi, at Chhatarpur village. They began to do farming here. On taking up this project, Lakshmi Chand Jain entrusted the charge of the refugee camp at Hudson Lines to others and himself settled down at Chhatarpur to provide facilities for farming to refugees by way of manure, seeds and other assistance.

In this activity even Pandit Nehru showed deep involvement. The Central Government in New Delhi decided to convert the Indian Cooperative Union into a cottage industry and named it Cottage Industries Emporium. Jain and Kamaladevi made this Emporium a centre for encouraging sale of handicrafts. Jain placed the products in the market through 'social marketing' while keeping an eye on the type of products that sold easily and those which were slow sellers. On the basis of his findings, the craftsmen began to produce goods and improve their products. In a survey conducted in 1953-54, Jain's old colleague, Raj Krishna revealed that the production of Indian handicrafts was to the tune of 6 million dollars per year. The production kept on showing an upward trend over the years.

The Cottage Industries Emporium, running through the combined efforts of Lakshmi Chand Jain and Kamaladevi Chattopadhyay, had a dramatic experience. In those days, Jayaprakash Narayan and Vinoba Bhave were engaged in the *bhoodan* (gift of land) movement. This pertains to the year 1954. Incidentally they ran into Lakshmi Chand Jain and none could find the answer on how to distribute the *bhoodan* land among the landless. Lakshmi Chand Jain found the question very challenging and got lost in finding an answer. After a long contemplation, he conveyed to Kamaladevi Chattopadhyay that he wanted to work with Vinoba Bhave. She quietly handed over the keys of the Emporium to a colleague, saying, "Shut down the Emporium. From today onwards the Emporium will remain closed. Lakshmi Chand Jain wants to leave and without him the Emporium cannot run."

For some time Lakshmi Chand Jain stood dumbstruck and then gave up the idea of leaving.

In 1968, Lakshmi Chand Jain started a consultancy firm which on the advice of farmers and craftspersons began to assist in governmental and non-governmental activities. This way Lakshmi Chand Jain helped in playing the role of a bridge between farmers, craftspersons and wokers' groups on the one hand and government committees and the Crafts Board on the other, with both duly benefiting from such a move.

K.V. SUBBANNA

Awarded for Journalism, Literature and Creative Communication Arts (1991)

Of late an increasing demand for village craft and handicrafts is seen among the rich urban elite of Asia who show off their creativity by displaying a glimpse of village in their urban homes. Similarly, folk songs, folk dance and folk art are finding space in towns and cities through the medium of television. This is a good sign but the reason for concern is that the display of different forms of art developed and displayed in cities is not reaching the village where the rural populace can enjoy its benefits. K.V. Subbanna noticed this aspect and realised that the villagers should be allowed to play a role in recitals of modern drama, music and films. Through concerted effort and understanding, he laid the foundation of the Neerasam Theatre Institute. He made world-level plays and films available in the mother tongue of the rural people of Karnataka. He won the Magsaysay Award of 1991 for enriching rural Karnataka with the world's best films and the delight and wonder of the living stage.

Though films, dances and plays appear on television which has reached many villages of India today, but the finer elements of urban culture are rarely introduced to the villagers. By introducing modern plays and films to rural folk in south India, K.V. Subbanna made a powerful case for the universality of art.

K.V. Subbanna was born on 24 January 1932 at Heggodu village on the Western Ghats of Mysore (now in Karnataka). The language spoken in the region was Kannada and the inhabitants did farming of coconut and arecanut. K.V. Subbanna's father, K.V. Ramappa, and mother, Savitramma K.V., belonged to a prosperous family. Rice farming was being done since long in their home.

Subbanna's initial education was carried out at home. His father brought him primary school textbooks in Kannada language and told him to "read it". They instructed him informally whenever they had time and he memorised the Sanskrit *mantras* and hymns in the Havyaka Brahma repertoire that were repeated daily in the house. In any case, his parents were in the know of the demand for a responsible government and Independence then sweeping India.

Subbanna's formal education began in 1943. About 10 kms away from his village there were a public middle and a high school in Sagar district. He started studying there. Though the medium of instruction was Kannada, Subbanna learned English too because of which he developed an interest in reading a lot of Western classics. Apart from these interests, Subbanna was a student of Science and Mathematics. While living at Sagar, he used to participate in plays held both in school and outside and never missed the opportunity to watch one either.

Since childhood Subbanna had been watching the traditional form of theatre called Yakshagana. Puranic literature and excerpts taken from the *Ramayana* and the *Mahabharata* were presented in Sanskrit. Apart from this, the annual month-long festival of drama form called 'proscenium theatre' and a reminiscent of Parsi theatre

was held at Sagar. The colourful, highly stylised melodramas, based on stories from such diverse sources as those of Shakespeare and the *Arabian Nights,* adapted to Indian tastes, were immensely popular.

After passing high school, Subbanna returned home. By then the country had achieved Independence. Subbanna was filled with enthusiasm at the new environment. He felt unusually restless, overwhelmed with a desire to do something new. Taking along some of his young friends, he formed a group at an isolated spot in Heggodu and started publishing a newspaper. The newspaper was titled *Ashoka Weekly* of which 500 copies were cyclostyled and distributed to highlight local news. This group, along with newspaper, started a drama organisation. Long before, there had been a group which used to perform the Yakshagana but had to close down due to some reasons. Subbanna decided to revive this club where he planned to stage both new and old plays. The youngsters discussed their plan at home. Subbanna's father became the first director of the newly formed drama company which was named after a local God – Nikanteshwara Natya Sewa Sangh, and it came to be called Ninasam, in short.

Subbanna became engrossed in his studies with like-minded friends who were interested in literature. However, his obsession with theatre continued unabated.

A very rich ambience for Kannada literature was present in Mysore University because eminent writer and award-winner poet K.V. Puttappa was teaching as a professor in the Literature Department. Under his supervision, Subbanna developed a deep understanding of literature. He understood the finer nuances of comparative literature and the relationship between literature and culture on the basis of Sanskrit, Islamic-Urdu and folk impressions. He could also establish their relationship with the theatre and was so encouraged that with the cooperation of his university friends, he founded a drama club. This club presented three to four new plays every year including those by Henrik Ibsen and George Bernard Shaw.

On leaving the university, Subbanna again returned to his village in 1954. He and his friends got together and revived the theatre company all over again. This time Subbanna tried to present modern plays just as he had staged at Mysore University. However, this experience proved disappointing. The rural population was still used to seeing musical plays based on *Puranic* tales presented in colourful costumes and with lots of action. Such a clientele did not find the new theatre enticing. Even then, Subbanna did not accept defeat and tried a new experiment. He tried presenting modern plays in the same craft to which the rural population was attracted. In this way, keeping their interest in mind, Subbanna created space for new themes.

In 1952, when Subbanna was studying in the university, the First International Film Festival was organised through concerted efforts of Jawahar Lal Nehru. On the occasion, three films – '*The Bicycle Thief*', '*Bitter Rice*' and '*Rashomon*' were screened in Mysore. On seeing these, Subbanna was greatly influenced and realised the strength of this medium. In 1955, when Satyajit Ray's film '*Pather Panchali*' was released, Subbanna made arrangements for its screening at Sagar. He even took his friends from Neenasam to see the film. In those days the facility of a projector had not yet reached his village Heggodu.

On 3 March 1956, Subbanna got married to Shailaja and after three years he became the father of a son, whom he named Akshara. In 1958, he even started a publishing house in the name of his son.

In 1963, Subbanna and his friends helped in the establishment of a college at Sagar and it was called Lal Bahadur College. In this college Subbanna worked for four years. At the same time, a club was formed to screen art films. In 1967, the UNESCO organised a film appreciation course at Poona. Subbanna studied this course and during its tenure of six weeks, he saw films by some top masters of the world.

In 1967 Subbanna returned again to work for his Ninasam. He fully devoted himself to expansion of his project. He included plays that children would appreciate. Meanwhile, along with this development, some female artistes too began to participate in plays and this enhanced Ninasam's reputation. In 1971, Subbanna had the desire to convert Ninasam into a full-fledged theatre. He discussed this with Karnataka's Finance Minister. Ramakrishna Hegde was the Finance Minister at that stage. He agreed on the condition that half the expenses would be incurred by the theatre company. This was sufficient. In 1972, a permanent theatre was constructed at Heggodu. It was called the Shivaram Karanth Rang Mandir. With the setting up of this theatre, apart from staging dramas, Subbanna received permission to screen films. He began to show a new kind of drama and films by Satyajit Ray, Akira Kurosawa, Sergei Eisenstein, Federico Fellini and others. .

Subbanna again began to stage international and other plays in Kannada for the people of Heggodu. He even translated regional language plays and published them at his press. He also began to train young boys and girls of his village and in 1980 established the Ninasam Theatre Institute for this purpose.

In 1983, Ninasam received a new boost when in collaboration with the Ford Foundation a new project titled 'Janaspandana' was started. It was a two-year project whose prime objective was to attract and enrich as many people as possible towards the theatre culture.

In 1991, K.V. Subbanna was awarded the Magsaysay Award for his contribution to rural theatre. In 1994, the Sangeet Natak Akademi awarded him for his exceptional contributions. In 2004, he received the Padma Shri from the Government of India.

In July 2005, K.V. Subbanna left this world.

PANDIT RAVI SHANKAR

Awarded for Journalism, Literature and Creative Communication Arts (1992)

Ragas *occupy a special position in the Indian tradition of vocal and instrumental music. Different types of* ragas *are played at different times and according to different seasons as they have the ability to express any form of sentiment. The more emotional the impact of the* raga *is, the more difficult it is to be learnt and presented. Pandit Ravi Shankar learned the finer nuances of the* ragas *through the medium of the* sitar *and mesmerised the whole world by playing it to them. Where* raga *is concerned, Ravi Shankar is "a thorough grammarian", said one of his admirers. Pandit Ravi Shankar was awarded the Magsaysay Award of 1992 for his exceptional talent for enriching India and the world with his sublime mastery of the* sitar *and with music "that colours the mind".*

The *raga* is music that colours the mind, so believed the ancient Indians. The well-rendered melody of a *raga* can convey ecstasy

and sorrow, sunlight and rain, dawn and twilight – any mood in man, or woman, or in Nature.

Pandit Ravi Shankar was born on 7 April 1920 in Benaras (now called Varanasi) in a Bengali Brahmin family. His family originally belonged to East Bengal which after Partition, became East Pakistan and is now known as Bangladesh.

Ravi Shankar's elder brother, Uday Shankar was a dancer. As a consequence, Pandit Ravi Shankar learnt to dance initially. What is more, in 1939, his first dance performance was held on the stage in front of a large audience.

Pandit Ravi Shankar acquired thorough grounding in music at a very young age. Baba Allauddin Khan was his *ustad* (teacher) who came to be known for establishing the Maihar *gharana* in Hindustani classical music. Ravi Shankar became his *guru's* favourite pupil, married his daughter, and after seven-and-a-half years of ceaseless training, left for Bombay in 1944 to establish his career.

In 1946, Pandit Ravi Shankar began creating music freely and even gave music in films, by recording his music with HMV's Indian affiliate. In 1956, Pandit Ravi Shankar was appointed the music director for All India Radio.

Soon Ravi Shankar's fame in *sitar* reached other countries and in 1954, he gave his first recital in the Soviet Union. In 1956, he received the chance to play the *sitar* in front of Western audiences. During this period, Ravi Shankar gave *sitar* recitals at Monterey Pop Festival and at the Royal Festival Hall.

In 1969, Pandit Ravi Shankar wrote his autobiography in English and titled it *My Music My Life*. In this, he highlighted many aspects of his life.

At the Woodstock Festival in California, Ravi Shankar was invited to present his *sitar* recital in 1969. Ustad Allah Rakha accompanied him on the *tabla*. In 1971, Pandit Ravi Shankar met George Harrison of the Beatles fame. He was one of the organisers of a musical meet to raise funds for Bangladesh. Ravi Shankar

and Harrison combined together to organise relief aid programmes which took the former to America in 1974. His final working album with Harrison was on a 1997 album, *Chants of India*, where Harrison developed an interest in chant music. Following Harrison's death in November 2001, Ravi Shankar attended a concert in London, dedicating the memorial to Harrison.

Ravi Shankar was critical of some facets of the West's reaction to Indian music. On a trip to San Francisco's Haight-Ashbury district after performing in Monterey, he wrote, "I felt offended and shocked to see India being regarded so superficially and its great culture being exploited. Yoga, *tantra*, *mantra*, *kundalini*, *ganja*, hashish, *Kama Sutra*, they all became a part of a cocktail that everyone seemed to be lapping up."

Pandit Ravi Shankar was a musician who was firmly disciplined to a life that the *ragas* called for. Despite staying within the limits of music, he gave birth to many new musical streams.

Pandit Ravi Shankar's music is kept recorded in many discs whose importance is considered equal to that of books. In 1956, his album titled, *Three Ragas* was released. A collection of his music on *sitar* was included in the disc, *Ragas and Talas* in 1964. The collection of his records of different *sitar* recitals and of his select *ragas* now totals nearly forty. The eminence of his music was revealed in his disc, *Tan-man* made in 1987, his autobiography, *The Man and His Music* in 2005 and another disc, *Flowers of India* in 2007.

Even in films, Ravi Shankar's music was found to be of world stature. The touch of his mastery is seen both in foreign films as also in Bengali. In 1966, Ravi Shankar composed the music for '*Alice in Wonderland*' under the Director, Jonathan Miller. Ravi Shankar provided music for Satyajit Ray's film, '*Apu's Triology*'. The music for Richard Attenborough's film '*Gandhi*' was composed by Ravi Shankar and so was the patriotic song '*Saare jahan se achcha…*'

Ravi Shankar has taught students in India and abroad. Significant contributions have been made in Indian music by Kartik

Kumar, Deepak Chowdhury, Harihar Rao, Amiya Dasgupta, Shamim Ahmed, Vishwa Mohan Bhatt and many others who have grown in stature, carrying on the legacy of Ravi Shankar.

His daughter, Anoushka Shankar, born in 1981, from his third wife, began learning the *sitar* from him at the age of eight. She has travelled both within and outside the country with him. She has held the audience spellbound with the art that she has acquired from her father. His second daughter, Norah Jones, from his second, Sue Jones, born in 1979, will also take his art forward received from him in legacy.

Pandit Ravi Shankar has won many awards. He has been honoured with honorary doctorates from fourteen different institutes. Padma Vibhushan and 'Desikottam' have been awarded to him. He was given the Grammy Award three times. He has received the Fukuoka Asian Culture Prize (Grand Prix) from Japan. He was honoured with the title 'Global Ambassador' and the Crystal Award from Davos.

In 1982, he shared with George Fenton the Academy Award for Best Original Score for the film '*Gandhi*'. In 1986, he was appointed a member of the Rajya Sabha where he stayed for six years. In 1998, Ravi Shankar shared with Ray Charles the Polar Music Prize. In 1999 he was honoured with the highest civilian honour, the Bharat Ratna. In 2002 he was conferred on the inaugural Indian Chamber of Commerce Lifetime Achievement Award.

BANOO JEHANGIR COYAJI

Awarded for Public Service (1993)

Banoo Jehangir Coyaji belonging to a Parsi family of Maharashtra, entered the field of medicine as a qualified doctor but her interest lay in the health of the rural poor women. These women were not only financially poor but also unaware of the importance of their health on account of being illiterate. Banoo Jehangir also observed that their status in society was that of a subordinate. In such a situation Dr Banoo's attention was drawn to the health of women and by choosing a hospital in Poona as her field of activity, she made an important contribution to improving the life of the rural women and their families in Maharashtra. Banoo Jehangir Coyaji was awarded the Magsaysay Award of 1993 for mobilising the resources for a modern urban hospital to bring better health and bright hopes to Maharashtra's rural women and their families.

Even today in the 21st century, many rural women in India die well beyond the pale of rudimentary health services, not to mention

modern medical technology. This is primarily due to rampant poverty, physical isolation and their subordinate position as females in the social order. Dr Banoo Coyaji confronted this cruel state of affairs in Maharashtra and was deeply affected by it.

Banoo was born in Bombay on 7 September 1917 and was the only daughter of her parents. Her Parsi family lived in Bombay where her father, Pestonji Kapadia, was a civil engineer and a *vaastu* specialist. Due to her birth in a rich family she was brought up in the lap of luxury. Her parents sent her to her grandparents in Poona as they feared that being their only child, she may get spoilt. Her grandparents' house was large, bursting with people, including servants and family retainers. "We used to sit down for a meal of twenty, twenty-five at a time," Banoo Coyaji once said. She received not only proper education at Poona but was also brought up well. Her parents used to visit her often from Bombay and "I never felt deprived," admitted Banoo.

At Poona, Banoo had her education at the Convent of Jesus & Mary for nine years till Senior Cambridge. She constantly stood first in her class. While studying in the Convent, Banoo learnt Western classical music for years, acquitting herself admirably before the external examiners from London's Trinity College of Music. Her maternal grandfather had a piano in the house. She developed a love for music which she received as a legacy from her father.

The Parsis strongly identified themselves with the British. In 1921 when the Prince of Wales visited Bombay, Banoo's father composed a welcome song for him but the family was nationalist at heart. Even as a child of four, she recalled, looking out from the sixth flooor of "my grandfather's house in Bombay and seeing the streets burning and hooliganism. And then Gandhiji arrived and there was peace while he was there."

After clearing her Cambridge examination with distinction in five subjects, Banoo decided to become a doctor. In 1993, she joined the St. Xaviers College in Bombay for her pre-medical classes.

She acquired her medical degree from the Grant Medical Collegke at Bombay. In 1940, she earned her M.D. degree from the same college.

Once in the year 1935, she happened to be spending her holidays in Mahabaleshwar. This hill station lies in the south of Maharashtra. She met Jehangir Coyaji, the younger brother of her idol and mentor over here. He had just returned from Purdue University after completing his engineering course. Banoo began to refer to Jehangir Coyaji as a boiler-maker from Purdue. Their involvement with each other grew and their courtship continued for five years. After obtaining her medical degree, Banoo got married to Jehangir Coyaji on 24 February 1941.

Soon after marriage, Banoo completed her residency (house job) in gynaecology under the direction of the esteemed Dr V.N. Shirodkar. During this period she gave birth to a son on 7 August 1942. Her son, Kurus, was the only child of his parents born through caesarean section.

In 1943, Bano and her husband Jehangir built their house in Poona. Jehangir was employed with the Poona Electric Supply Company. On reaching Poona, instead of practicing gynaecology, Banoo chose to work as an ordinary physician with Dr Edulji Coyaji. She constantly said, "I am a gynaeocolgist by profession but I am a general practitioner at heart."

One day her husband Jehangir, all of a sudden announced that from the next day she had to start working at the King Edward Memorial hospital (KEM). On further enquiry, it was discovered that the hospital's Chairman, Sardar Mudaliar had personally invited Banoo to join the hospital. He wanted a skilful doctor urgently. Accepting the proposal, Banoo took charge as doctor at KEM on 14 May 1944.

The KEM hospital had been established in Poona in 1912 in memory of King Edward VII who had died that year. It was a private charity hospital subsisting on a small endowment and

donations. When Banoo set foot in the hospital, there were only 40 beds. Since the hospital's only other doctor was on sick leave, she had to take charge immediately. Most the of KEM patients were poor Hindu women. Although KEM hospital was primarily meant for attending to gynaecological cases, the poor women feared going to any other hospital and only went there when they were desperate. Arriving in carts from villages, they came when in labour pains, or tooth abscess, or with an infected appendix. Medical Director, Banoo Coyaji, and another female doctor plus three nurses made up KEM's entire professional staff. To meet the demands, they often worked eighteen hours a day, doing everything.

By the time Banoo Coyaji joined KEM, her Pune grandparents had died and the big house where she had been brought up was sold out. So she with Jehangir and Kurus moved into an apartment built right on top of the hospital. The arrangement was convenient for Banoo. She used to attend to her son also while working for long hours at the hospital. Jehangir's office too was across the road. Thus the arrangement was "very comfortable for me." Despite the long hours at the hospital Banoo thrived.

It had been three years after joining KEM hospital that the country's long political struggle came to an end. This struggle had never been far from her thoughts. One particular incident of 1942 she always remembered with great warmth. Once, during the holidays, she happened to be at a family's house situated on the seacoast of Bulsar. There she and her maternal cousins noticed Gandhiji strolling on the coast. At that time Banoo was merely a child. During that period, Gandhiji was collecting donations for the Harijans. On noticing Gandhiji, Banoo and her sisters rushed to meet him. Gandhiji asked them, "From where have you all come?"

They pointed in the direction of their house.

At this Gandhiji asked them, "In that case, you all must be very rich?"

"Yes!" agreed Banoo.

"Then go and get Rs 100 each for the Harijan Fund..."

On hearing his, Banoo along with her sisters ran home and pestered her maternal aunt and uncle to donate towards the Harijan Fund. The next day Banoo took Rs 100 from them and donated it to the Fund happily.

When the country became independent, Jehangir saw the Union Jack being lowered and the tricolour being raised high on the flagpole. "I don't cry easily, but there were tears rolling down my eyes and my husband's eyes when we saw that," she admitted.

Till the decade of 1960, Banoo worked devotedly at KEM but then she realised that it was not enough to complete her daily work with limited staff. She put forth a proposal for extending the services of KEM to the villages. She said, "Patients would come to my door, seriously ill, dying, or in carts with one baby delivered and the other baby still inside, or with an arm sticking out. It was a very sad thing," she reflected. While exploring the possibilities, she was encouraged by the great educationist J.P. Naik. Banoo's eyes fell on Vadu block where 30,000 villagers lived in some twenty-two isolated hamlets across a dry drought-prone terrain. She asked the Health Secretary of the state government to hand over the primary health unit to her to let her run it. The startled official readily agreed. In 1972, a small outpatient clinic was set up in Vadu, where facilities were provided for maternal and child care plus family planning.

Banoo understood the dire need for a family planning programme. This was the need of the hour as the illiterate rural women had many children whose upbringing was difficult on account of poverty. It was 1975 and Prime Minister Indira Gandhi invoked the Emergency which was seriously criticised by Banoo. She was absolutely against Mrs. Gandhi's population control campaign. Probably her criticisms were converyed to Mrs. Gandhi, who invited Banoo to meet her personally. Banoo met her and place forth her proposals for the family planning programme.

Meanwhile her project at Vadu started facing many problems and after introducing many revolutionary measures, the clinic at Vadu began to funcion properly. She ofen loved to quote Prime Minister Jawahar Lal Nehru who had said, "To awaken people, it is the woman who must be awakened. Once she is on the move, the family moves, the village moves, the nation moves."

In 1989, Banoo was awarded the Padma Bhushan. On 15 July 2004, Banoo Coyaji left for heavenly abode.

KIRAN BEDI

Awarded for Public Service (1994)

Kiran Bedi's name as the first Indian woman to join the Indian Police Service (IPS) created waves in 1972 and since then on her journey from the Indian Police Service to the United Nations Organisation, she has worked on important, and sometimes dangerous, postings. She worked in the United Nations as the Police Advisor to the Secretary-General in the Department of Peace-keeping Operations. When on the one hand she set an example by being a firm and fearless officer, on the other, she revealed the just and emotional aspect of her personality when running the Tihar Jail. Here she even altered the lifestyle of the prisoners. Kiran Bedi was awarded the Magsaysay Award of 1994 for building confidence in India's police through dynamic leadership and effective innovations in crime control, drug rehabilitation and humane prison reforms.

No social relationship is more fraught with ambiguity than that between the police and the public. Maintaining order and public

safety while making the traffic run smoothly, is what Kiran Bedi had to do.

Born on 9 June 1949 at Amritsar in the house of her father Prakash Lal Peshawaria and mother Premlata, Kiran had her entire education, from school till graduation, at Amritsar itself. She received her Masters degree in political science from the Punjab University and LLB from Delhi University. In 1993, she obtained her Ph.D. (doctorate) from the Social Science Department of IIT (Delhi).

Kiran Bedi was not only a bright student but also obsessed with playing tennis. In 1972, she won the Asian Lawn Tennis Championship for women. The very same year she entered the Indian Police Academy from where she emerged as a full-fledged police officer in 1974.

Prior to entering the police service, Kiran Bedi began her career as a lecturer from 1970 to 1972, while preparing for the Indian Administrative Services. She suffered some setbacks in life which have made her all the more sensitive and determined. Kiran Bedi's elder sister Shashi got married to a heart specialist settled in Canada. When she went to join her husband abroad, she discovered that the doctor was already living with another woman. This situation was tolerated silently by Shashi for long but this incident made Kiran especially cautious in life.

As a result of her over-cautiousness, Kiran Bedi took two major decisions. She revealed that when entering into a matrimonial alliance with a prospective groom she found that he considered her career of no importance and so she was forced to reject him. The second time, the prospective groom's family was very orthodox and which apart from rites and rituals was interested in getting a dowry. Kiran rejected even this proposal.

In 1972, Kiran fell in love with Raj Bedi on the tennis court and both got married in a temple without any pomp and show. Kiran and Raj were ambitious and for both their field of activity was more important than their personal life. In such a situation,

both of them decided to lead independent lives, though their emotional bond continues. In her moments of loneliness, Kiran takes refuge in poetry. She continues her mental bond with her husband. She has a daughter Sania who has married a journalist, R.B. Bharuch, who also produces films.

Kiran Bedi has occupied many important posts during her career in the police service. In 1977, she single-handedly drove off a band of club-and-sword-wielding demonstrators with her police baton. This was the encounter between the Akalis and the Nirankaris at India Gate in Delhi. In 1979, she became Deputy Commissioner of Police and was given charge of west Delhi. She completely eradicated the illegal trade in liquor which had been flourishing since past 200 years in this area and suggested to the bootleggers to adopt alternative modes of employment for earning their livelihood.

In 1981, on becoming Deputy Commissioner (Traffic) became an important landmark in her career. In 1982, the Asian Games was held in Delhi. Not only from nearby, but also from all over the country and abroad spectators gathered in Delhi and it seemed as though a flood of cars had descended upon Delhi. The Delhi administration increased the strength of its transport and other vehicles and in such a situation handling the traffic proved a very challenging job.

While enforcing discipline and strict observance of the code of conduct for smooth functioning of the traffic, Kiran Bedi made some enemies. However, she continued to work extensively for the welfare of the employees of the police service. In 1985, she was appointed Deputy Commissioner (DCP) in the secretariat. Within one day of joining, she issued orders for promotion of long-pending cases of 1,600 employees.

Whichever department she worked in, Kiran Bedi's work remained exemplary and she was highly praised. While attending to her responsibilities Kiran set an example by revealing her brave

personality. In 1984, Indira Gandhi as the Prime Minister had to go abroad for some urgent work. Her car had to be taken to the garage for repair and was parked on the wrong side of the road. In those days, Kiran's rule was at its height and she got the car towed away by the crane. It was only after paying the fine that the vehicle was released to the owner. Government vehicles too were not spared from the rod of Kiran. As a result, Kiran Bedi's came to be known as 'Crane Bedi'. However, it had no effect on her.

Kiran Bedi's tenure in 1993 is said to be the most remarkable one. She was appointed as IG (Prisons), when she decided to convert Tihar into an ideal prison. She took steps to make the jail convicts more civilised and humane. She said that she would convert the prison into an *ashram*. She began organising classes in *yoga*, *dhyana*, *vipassana*, apart from sports activities and cultural programmes. Classes were organised to teach the inmates to read and write. Drug addiction was brought under control through kindness.

Among the 10,000 prisoners in jail, she found that most of them had no charge filed against them but had been kept imprisoned for years. Kiran Bedi attended not only to their physical health but also mental growth. Prisoners appeared for their examination from within the prison walls and increased their educational qualifications. The prisoners were allowed to attend poetry and *mushaira* programmes. Kiran was immensely praised for this revolutionary effort of hers.

Kiran Bedi occupied the post of Director-General at the Indian Bureau of Research and Development in the police department. She also became the police advisor of the peace-keeping forces of the UN.

Apart from her government duties, Kiran Bedi now runs two organisations --- Navjyoti, a crèche in Tihar Jail and India Vision Foundation which is engaged in reformation of drug addicts. Her NGOs reach out to over 10,000 beneficiaries daily in areas

of drug abuse treatment, schooling of children of prisoners in addition to education, training, counselling and health care of the urban and rural poor. For her efforts in trying to control addiction and rehabilitate addicts, the United Nations Organisation presented her the Surge Sortik Memorial Award. This award was given to her NGO Navjyoti on 28 June 1999.

In polls conducted by *The Week*, a weekly magazine, Krian Bedi was voted as the most admired woman in the country and as one of the 15 Indian icons of 2006.

For her commendable contributions, Kiran Bedi has won many awards and honours. In 1979, she won the President's Gallantry Award; in 1980, she was selected 'Woman of the Year'; in 1995, she won the 'Father Mashismo Award'; in 1997 she was declared the 'Lion of the Year'; and in 1999, she was declared the 'Pride of India'. In the year 2005, she was honoured with the 'Mother Teresa National Award for Social Justice'.

Kiran Bedi has written many books, among which a series of books have been published under the title *What I Saw*, where woman power and Indian police have been highlighted. *I Dare* is her autobiography in which she has placed forth many of her life experiences.

Kiran Bedi has now retired and features in a regular programme on television besides running two NGOs.

PANDURANG SHASTRI ATHAVALE

Awarded for Community Leadership (1996)

There is a treasure-trove of knowledge on India in the Vedas *and the* Upanishads. *India's ancient sages conveyed a view of the cosmos so complex and compelling that it survives vibrantly till today. What is more, enriched with newer religions over centuries, the Hindu civilisation pervades the life of modern India. Pandurang Shastri Athavale has realised this aspect and is drawing strength for his country's spiritual renewal and material uplift. Based on this knowledge and information, he is trying to bring about a change in the society. Pandurang Shastri Athavale was awarded the 1996 Magsaysay Award for tapping the ancient well-springs of Hindu civilisation to inspire spiritual renewal and social transformation in modern India.*

Pandurang Shastri Athavale in one of his sermons said, "God resides in everyone and achieving spiritual oneness" will bring with it solutions for worldly problems.

Pandurang was born on 19 October 1920 in a Brahmin family at Roha near Bombay. Endowed with religious zeal, Pandurang's family was steeped in the tradition of erudition. Carrying this talent forward, he acquired knowledge of Sanskrit language and got down to studying the Hindu epics.

Pandurang through self-encouragement launched a self-learning movement which was based on the *Bhagwad Gita.* Self-education encouraged Pandurang to utilise the knowledge obtained through self-learning to solve social and economic problems. By establishing a relationship between experience and maturity and through self-learning he propagated its importance in society and presented a solution to many problems.

In 1954, Pandurang received the opportunity to participate in the Second World Religious Conference at Shimatsu, Japan. At this conference, he expounded on the importance of Vedic knowledge and philosophy of life while emphasising the need for putting it into practice. At the conference, a person from the audience got up and asked, "In our country is there a single community that lives by these ideals?"

This question disturbed him immensely. He quietly returned to India and began to ponder on the grim realities of contemporary Indian life.

He founded a school in 1956 where India's sacred knowledge combined with Western learning was taught. He named the institute Tatva Gyan Vidyapeeth. He began to meet regularly groups of earnest young truth-seekers, entrepreneurs, doctors, engineers and lawyers. He taught them the message of enriching the soul through the self-awareness (*swadhyaya*) movement. This movement is gaining strength day by day and Pandurang Shastri Athavale is addressed as '*Dada*' (elder brother) among his devotees. He has tried to introduce a philosophy in society by which people despite their busy life could find time to meditate on God and inculcate the spirit of *Bhakti.*

During his campaign in 1958, Athavale and his volunteers took tours to thousands of villages to spread his message while expounding upon the power of the *swadhyaya* movement. In hundreds of villages, *swadhyaya* devotees have abandoned drunkenness, gambling, wife-beating and petty crimes to devote themselves to community welfare. The scene in villages has undergone a marked change. Fisherfolk chant Sanskrit hymns and ply 'boat temples' whose daily catch is reserved for the local hungry. Villagers plant multi-hectare 'tree temples' to restore degraded land and stop deforestation. Farmers cultivate their fields as 'God's farms' to grow food to share with needy neighbours. *Swadhyaya*-imbued villages are clean, tidy and prosperous. Children regularly attend school. Untouchability is not practiced anywhere and there is no communal strife. Muslims, Hindus and Christians share the same place of worship.

Athavale often tells the people that *swadhyaya* has nothing to do with politics cannot solve the problems of the world. "We are merely planting a bouquet of flowers of love, compassion, selflessness and peace."

A small organisation of volunteers gives some coordination to Athavale's vast 'family' and guides the work of *swadhyaya* schools. It is largely through his teachings that he leads the movement. His pithy, conversational sermons hold multitudes in rapt attention. He exhorts his listeners to liberate themselves from preconceived ideas and "baseless beliefs". He asserts, "The basic revolution should be of the human mind."

In 1988, Dada Pandurang was awarded the Mahatma Gandhi Award. On 19 March he addressed his devotees in a large gathering that met at Rajkot. In 1997, Pandurang was awarded the Templeton Award for the development of his field.

On 25 October 2003 Dada Pandurang Shastri Athavale took leave from this world.

T.N. SESHAN

Awarded for Public Service (1996)

On taking up government employment through the Indian Administrative Service (IAS), T.N. Seshan worked in various ministries and departments of the state and Central Government. In December 1990, he took charge as the tenth Chief Election Commissioner and remained on this post till 1996. During this period, Seshan introduced many changes in the electoral process to ensure independent and free elections. In this period, he had to face stiff opposition from political leaders and government officials, but he did not waver. He kept on trying to introduce his decisions fearlessly. With his concerted efforts the democratic system got strengthened and the voter began to place confidence in the sysem. Seshan was awarded the Magsaysay Award of 1996 for his resolute actions to bring order, fairness and integrity to elections in India, the world's largest democracy.

India with its huge population, is Asia's most diverse democracy. T.N. Seshan felt that India's democracy had grave flaws as "it is

a government of some people, for some people, by some people." He decided to bring about a change in whatever way he could.

Tirunellai Narayana Iyer Seshan was born on 15 May 1933 at Tirunellai village of Palghat (also spelled as Palakkad) district in Kerala. Seshan's family of Brahmins came from the southern tip of India and travelled westwards to Kerala in search of water, before settling down at Palghat some 400 years ago. Palghat then comprised ninety-two Brahmin villages called *agraharams*. According to Seshan, "Palghat Brahmins came to excel in four fields – as civil servants and musicians, cooks and crooks." His father was a lawyer. His law practice made it necessary for the family to move from their home village of Tirunellai to the town of Palghat, which was the administrative centre for the sub-district. T.N. Seshan was the youngest among his six brothers and sisters. He classified his family as belonging to the "bottom quarter of the middle class."

Seshan had his early education at Basel Evangelical Mission High School at Palghat. This school had been started by a Swiss missionary. In the decade of the forties, Seshan passed his high school. He was considered a 'bookworm' and an 'introvert' at school. As a bookworm he described his life as "hostel morning, evening and night." He was fond of playing chess but was not interested in physical exercise. High school was followed by an intermediate examination of two years which served as a 'bridge' to learning English language.

Seshan enjoyed physics and engineering subjects but also read Shakespeare, Wordsworth, Bacon and Byron. He chose science but after being refused admission to four engineering shools in the area, he decided to study physics at Madras Christian College, which was run by Scottish Presbyterian missionaries. He completed the syllabus for B.Sc. Honours degree in three years whereas the course was designed around a four-year syllabus.

In the early 1950s, Seshan worked for some time as a scientist. He even taught in his college for three years from 1952-1955 but

left his job due to the "pathetic" salary. In 1954, T.N. Seshan appeared for the Indian Administrative Service (IAS) examination and joined the civil service as a trainee.

From being a trainee at the Academy of Administration in Delhi, Seshan became Assistant Collector for one year at Coimbatore. His first posting as Sub-Collector at Dindigul in Madurai district of Tamil Nadu, allowed him to exercise his responsibilities as a "comprehensive executive", taking charge of water supply, revenue, judiciary and law and order. It was on this post that he showed his strong character by implementing the law despite interference from a politician. A Harijan married to the President of the local Congress Party was arrested on the charge of embezzlement. A minister on a visit to the area wanted the Harijan released, but Seshan refused to do so. He stood his ground despite being chastised and scorned by the communist-influenced villagers. Very adroitly not only did he save his job, but escaped without compromising his position.

In 1958, he was moved to Madras as Director of Programmes and Deputy Secretary in the Secretariat for Rural Development, a post he held for four years. He was put incharge of Panchayat work, where interference by local political leaders made his task difficult. Even his role as an IAS officer was reduced. In the end, Seshan observed, "The very people involved in administering the project conspired against its continuation."

It was during this period that Seshan married Jayalakshmi. What is strange is that Seshan's family believed in horoscope matching and Jayalakshmi's horoscope predicted that the marriage would be childless. Still Seshan married her in 1959, a month after they had first met.

In 1962, when he was in the Secretariat, he was ordered to supervise the small savings programme, the welfare of backward classes and women's welfare. Seshan worked with such deep devotion that his fame spread to all other departments. Seshan's reputation

as an officer even reached Ramaswami Venkataraman, the Minister for Transport and Heavy Industries. Seshan was appointed Director at the Transport Department. Venkataraman warned Seshan that the transport system in Madras was in shambles, but the latter should accept it as a challenge and bring about an improvement in it.

Accepting the challenge, Seshan took charge of supervising 4,000 employees and running 3,000 buses. For Seshan this was a most satisfying job and another training ground for higher responsibilities. The work required him to run "all kinds of things" and on occasions, even meet and defy crowds. He got so deeply involved in this work that once during a strike by bus-drivers he personally drove down a bus. He showed that he was not only an officer but capable of handling other things too. He worked here for two years and restored the system back on the rails. Seshan himself once said that he learnt many things on this job whose benefits he derived in the future too.

Seshan was appointed Collector at Madurai in December 1964. During this period he received the Ed Mason Scholarship from Harvard University. He left for North America with his wife, Jayalakshmi. Here he toured extensively and in 1968, acquired a degree in Public Administration. This period was a very relaxing time for him but the only problem was the food in America. Being a vegetarian, the food was not to his liking.

In 1969, on returning from abroad, Seshan got the opportunity to experience the prestige of one of the highest services in the Indian Government. Immediately on arrival, he was appointed head of the Atomic Energy Department, which was directly under the Prime Minister. He stayed on this post till 1976 and he admitted that it was here that he learned new management techniques, one of them being how "conflict can be used to generate results."

In 1976, Seshan returned to Tamil Nadu to serve concurrently as Secretary of Industries and Agriculture. But after a "massive

quarrel" with the Chief Minister of Tamil Nadu, he resigned and was shifted to Delhi as a member of the Oil and Natural Gas Commission. Seshan's continuous complaint was that there was political intereference in the civil administration and that "the current politicians are looting the State."

He was famous for speaking out his mind and often spoke bluntly. Once during his tenure, he called certain IAS officers as 'polaroid callgirls' who bowed down to the wishes of powerful officials and political leaders. He was also heard saying that he certainly was a vegetarian but he could swallow raw all the corrupt officers. Nevertheless, he never changed from vegetarianism, nor lost control over his conduct.

After two years, he took over as Additional Secretary in the Ministry of Space (from 1980-1985), participating in research activities due to his interest and knowledge of science and engineering. At Prime Minister Rajiv Gandhi's request, Seshan was brought to the Ministry of Forest and Environment as Cabinet Secretary (1985-1988). Seshan's close association with Rajiv Gandhi began when he was asked to investigate an attempt on the Prime Minister's life. Rajiv liked the report and asked Seshan to become Secretary of Internal Security, a post he held until 1989 in addition to continuing as Environment Secretary. After 1989, Seshan continued as Secretary in Ministry of Defence. He was named Cabinet Secretary. But Rajiv Gandhi lost the premiership in December 1989 and Seshan was given membership of the non-descript Planning Commission.

The new Prime Minister, Chandra Shekhar, offered Seshan the post of Chief Election Commissioner. Seshan's first impulse was to reject the offer, but after consulting Rajiv Gandhi and President R.Venkataraman, he took charge on 12 December 1990. Soon afterwards, Seshan began to introduce changes. First of all, he got pictures of gods and goddesses removed from the offices of the Election Department so as to present an image of secularism.

He restored office discipline, banned long lunch breaks and reading in the library during office hours.

In resolving electoral cases, Seshan acted swiftly. In a high-profile case he heard the case once and settled it. His predecessor had held multiple hearings and taken down 1,600 pages of notes without coming to a decision.

Since the task of holding national elections in a large country like India is gargantuan, many polling booths so far had been manned by temporarily deputed state employees. Seshan observed that many of the employees took their duties lightly. So he began cracking down on them. The state officials objected. Seshan argued that the state employees fell under his jurisdiction. The very authority of the Commission was at stake, he said. Many local bureaucrats were under the thumb of local politicians who had deputed their men to man the booths. For free and fair elections Seshan insisted on controlling the deputised personnel strictly. The fight went to Supreme Court which ruled in favour of Seshan's authority over the deputed personnel.

Seshan had to attend to three prime duties --- ensuring the autonomy and integrity of the Election Commission, empowerment of the voters, improvement in the electoral procedures and changes in the election laws.

Seshan began to work in all the three areas. Use of identity cards in the election process and curbs on expenditure by candidates and their parties were enforced strictly. This work was not easy. It was because of the absence of these measures that the path to corruption in elections lay open. Seshan's restrictions went against those who entered the election field by purchasing votes. Forcible occupation of voters' booths and violence were the other points over which Seshan imposed restrictions. Without any fear, Seshan entered the field.

In 1993, during the elections in Tamil Nadu, there seemed to be a likelihood of eruption of violence. It was necessary to

curb this violence for holding free and impartial elections. So Seshan asked for assistance of the armed forces from various state governments and hoped that all the state governments would come to his assistance. But the former Home Minister of State turned down the demand. At this, Seshan made the announcement that he would not hold the elections without fulfilment of his demand. A standoff resulted and it took the political leaders "by storm", according to Seshan. Seshan remained undaunted. He placed his stand in front of the Supreme Court. Before the Supreme Court could give any decision, Seshan rescinded his order banning elections. This tactical withdrawal earned him credit in the eyes of the electorate.

Meanwhile in October 1993, the Central Government by making amendments in the Constitution appointed two Additional Commissioners, M.S. Gill and Krishnamurty, to neutralise Seshan's independent streak. Both of them were the government's own men. This was found very unacceptable by Seshan. He again knocked on the doors of the Supreme Court. Granting interim relief, the Supreme Court said that Seshan was not bound to agree with the decisions of other two Commissioners. Even otherwise, the appointment of three Commissioners had never been seen before. Despite such pressures, Seshan continued to do his work. But ultimately, the Supreme Court ruled that the position of the Chief Commissioner vis-à-vis the two other Commissioners was "no more than that of the first among equals, that is, the principle of a majority rule should henceforth prevail." This decision was announced on 2 February 1996. On 11 December 1996, Seshan completed his tenure in the Election Commission and resigned.

Seshan now leads a modest life with his wife, brooding incessantly over the fate of India. Elections, in his view, constitute only one element of modern Indian life that needs "cleaning up". Despite all kinds of opposition and confrontations, Seshan's image as a trustworthy and devoted worker remains steadfast to this day.

He even submitted his papers for the post of the President of India. In reply to a question from journalists, he said, "I know I will not win. But I enjoy participating in a competition. Even in school, despite being a non-sportsperson, I competed in the Long Jump event."

MAHASWETA DEVI

Awarded for Journalism, Literature and Creative Communication Arts (1997)

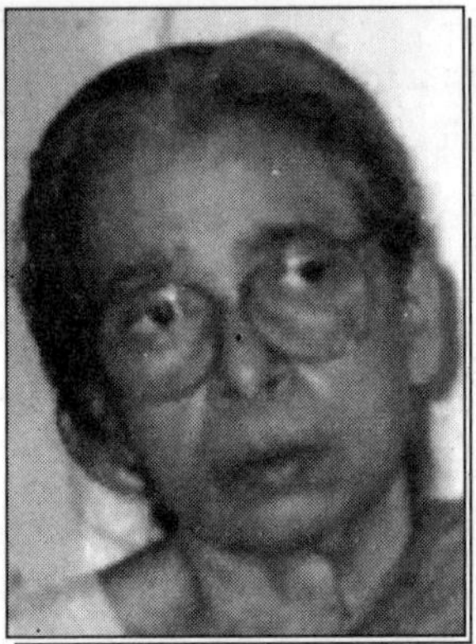

Mahasweta Devi believes in fighting for the rights of the marginalised people, including the Dalits and the Adivasis through her writings and social activism. A well-known name in Bengali literature, she has a deep understanding of the life of the Adivasis and the injustice meted out to them. She has made their life the theme of her writings and has learnt much by walking through Adivasi areas of Madhya Pradesh and Chhattisgarh. She is conscious of the pain of the Adivasis, the Dalits and the women, as they have been victims of injustice, oppression and exploitation since the time of the British. It was the British who branded the Adivasi criminals under the 1871 Criminal Tribes Act. She continues to fight for their rights against the administration and tries to get them their due justice and facilities. Mahasweta Devi has also worked towards making this class of people knowledgeable and self-reliant. She has objected to the government's employment and industrial policies and wants the Adivasis to become self-

reliant and capable. Mahasweta Devi was awarded the Magsaysay Award of 1997 for her compassionate crusade through art and activism to claim for tribal people a just and honourable place in India's national life.

Certain tribes of West Bengal, like the Lodha, the Kheria and Dhekaro (Shabars) were nomadic tribes, travelling from village to village as minstrels or acrobats, instead of pursuing a settled life. Though the Government of India identified these tribes in 1952, it made no provision for their livelihood and they continued to suffer the stigma of being 'criminal'. She said, "Even a new-born baby in these tribes was branded criminal by law...Age-old mindsets are difficult to change. Even today, they are treated like criminals in districts like Purulia, Medinipur, Birbhum, and Bankura."

Mahasweta Devi was born on 14 January 1926 in Dacca (now in Bangladesh) in a family of poets, writers and artists. As a child her personality was moulded in the rich milieu of Bengal's high culture. Her father, Manish Ghatak, was a poet and novelist and elder brother Ritwik Ghatak was a noted filmmaker. Her mother, Dharitri Devi, was also a writer and social worker. Thus Mahasweta acquired her creative and social leanings in legacy from her parents.

Mahasweta Devi's schooling began in Dacca but following the country's Partition, she came to West Bengal with the family. Here she graduated with English Honours from Santiniketan, Viswa-Bharati University. For doing postgraduation in English, she joined the Calcutta University and stood first in the examination.

In 1964, she began teaching at Bijoygarh College, which was an affiliated college of Calcutta Universtiy. This college is being run for working-class women by Calcutta University. While teaching, she also worked as a journalist and a creative writer. In the vast Bengali literature that she has written, she often depicts the brutal oppression of tribal people and the untouchables by potent, authoritarian, upper-caste landlords, money-lenders and venal

government officials. She started working among the Dalits and women to advice them on their rights. She is an activist who is dedicated to the struggles of tribals in Bihar, Madhya Pradesh and Chhattisgarh. Her attention was drawn more towards the tribal communities, the Lodha and Shabars.

On reaching the remote and impoverished district of Palamu in Bihar, in 1965, she called it "a mirror of India". Moving from place to place on foot, she witnessed the savage impact of absentee landlordism and debt-bondage on indigenous society, especially on women. In India's other tribal districts, too, she observed people leading a "sub-human existence." They had neither education nor health services, no road, no means to earn a livelihood. It was a heart-rending sight for her.

Mahasweta Devi, through the medium of her writing, began to depict the true picture of the life of the tribals. In the mid-1970s, her words zeroed in on the plight of tribals through the years and she calls them "the suffering spectators of the India traveling towards the 21st century."

Her first book *Hajar Churasi ki Maa* was published in 1975. Inspired by Calcutta's Naxalite movement in the late 1960s and 1970s, the story depicts the plight of a traumatised upper-middle class woman who learns that her son is lying dead in a police morgue owing to his involvement in the movement.

Mahasweta Devi intricately weaves contemporary scenes with indigenous and original historical subjects to reveal why the Adivasis are being tortured by India's dominating castes and the administration. In another story, *Aranyer Adhikar* (Right to the Forest,) published in 1977, she chronicles the life and struggles of tribal leader, Birsa Munda, in the late 19th century. Her book, *Dropdi* published in 1977, is the tale of Dropdi, a rebel who refuses to be subjugated despite being raped. Her book *Iter Parey It* in 1987 is about tribal women exploited at brick kilns.

In her stories, lives of real and living women are depicted

to show that there comes a day when continued suppression makes them revolt in revenge.

Along with creative writing, Mahasweta Devi's activities include confrontations with the administration. She has often written letters of complaint to the government against police atrocities, landlords, state leaders and Adivasis and got them published in newspapers when any issue pertaining to injustice or atrocity against the Adivasis is discovered. This way, like an obsession, she makes the affairs of the Adivasis her pet theme.

In the beginning of 1970, Mahasweta Devi began to intervene directly to issues related to the Adivasis and the administration. She gave full support to Adivasis and other victims, making them raise their combined voice to protest the hostility against them and demand their right to development and growth. She taught the extremely poor Adivasis of West Begal to grow trees, irrigate fields, make handicrafts, take care of their savings and observe cleanliness for health reasons through the Khediya Shabar Welfare Society. She suggested to them the path to learn how to read and write. She helped them organise annual fairs where they could exhibit their crafts and develop self-confidence. She founded many such societies and taught them how to work together.

She launched a movement against the industrial policies of West Bengal government which was unable to take care of the welfare of the people living on the edge. Mahasweta Devi set an example of this at Singur and Nandigram where land was acquired from the tribals to set up a chemical hub in collaboration with Indonesia's Salim Group. When the police entered Nandigram and fired at the villagers, leading to fourteen deaths, Mahasweta said, "Rich fertile land is being taken over forcefully by the government. Activists like Mamata [Banerjee] and Medha [Patekar] were already involved; I have just butted in."

Mahasweta Devi did a complete course in business management from Viswa-Bharati, Santiniketan and pointed out that

this institute was not started by Gurudev Tagore for the purpose of business. She recalled that she began her education at this place.

An incident from her life reveals her sensitivity. She was speaking at the inauguration of the Frankfurt Book Fair in 2006 when India was the first country to be invited as a guest nation for the second time. Undoubtedly, feelings of Indian nationalism ran high. She made an impassioned inaugural speech when she moved the audience to tears wih her lines taken from a famous film song by film star Raj Kapoor. She said, "It is the right time to say that my shoe is Japanese, trousers are English, hat on the head is Russian, that is, we are global, but the *dil* --- *dil* (heart) is always Hindustani (Indian). My India is torn, tattered, proud, beautiful, hot, humid, cold, sandy, shining India; my country."

Twenty-two important books have been written by her including *Aranyer Adhikar*, *Rudali* and others, some of which constitute the best in literature.

Mahasweta Devi received many important awards. In 1979 she was awarded the Sahitya Akademi Award and in 1996, the Jnanpith Award (which is considered equivalent to the Nobel Prize in India). She was honoured with the Padma Shri in 1986 and the Padma Vibhushan in 2006.

Mahasweta Devi continues to remain engaged in her task. She once replied to a journalist, who wanted to interview her, "Why should I give an interview? My work should speak for itself..." Her love for her country oozes out when she says, "I've been to many countries but every time, I want to come back even though many things have been bypassed since 1947. I can't live anywhere else. I just can't stand it. I belong to India. It's what gives me pride. If my mother was poor, skeletal and couldn't give me food, I would still be proud to call her my mother. It's like that. It's my country. It's my India."

MAHESH CHANDER MEHTA

Awarded for Public Service (1997)

The Constitution of India gives to the people equal rights to lead a normal life. But like other developing countries, India too is facing depletion of natural resources and degradation of the environment. Keeping this in mind, the law for protection of environment was introduced after Independence. It is, however, a cause for worry that this law is being flagrantly breached. Mahesh Chander Mehta made preservation of environment his cause and single-handedly got engrossed in fighting a legal battle. He filed cases against such indifference to protection of environment and won. He was awarded the Magsaysay Award of 1997 for claiming for India's present and future citizens their constitutional right to a clean and healthy environment.

Very little is being done to prevent the malignant discharges from cars from polluting the air, the water and the earth. As a result, crippling consequences are faced by India's crowded millions. The

crusading public-interest lawyer, Mahesh Chander Mehta's lament is that though environmental agencies do have teeth, "but they refuse to bite."

Mahesh Chander Mehta was born in 1942, shortly before the Partition of India. His birthplace is Sohana village in Jammu region. He was taken as a small child to Dhangri village as Sohana was not considered safe from trouble and strife in this border area of Jammu & Kashmir. He was brought up in a village surrounded by the Panchal ranges which he described as beautiful, hilly and not far from the Kashmir Valley. The languages spoken here were Dogri and Pakari.

The family was Brahmin and Mehta's father was a community leader, commanding great respect in the village of a hundred families or so for he was literate. The village school in which Mehta studied was a one-room tenement but with arrangements made by his father, facililties were provided for six students to sit on rugs spread on the ground. The blackboard was biodegradable. Mehta's father was the chief of the village Panchayat. He was conscious of the importance of preserving the environment.

Mahesh passed out from high school at the age of eighteen. His parents wanted to get him married but his desire was to teach in a village at Jammu. He considered it advisable not to remain dependent on his family but live independently by supporting himself. In this decision he even made it clear to his parents that no change would occur in his relationship with them.

Mahesh worked as an accountant in a shoe store. His friends encouraged him to start a coaching centre in which school children could study at night. Mahesh himself attended to teaching the children at this centre.

By 1970, Mahesh began to take interest in social work. During this period, he participated in many trainining camps and worked in villages. This work was done on behalf of the Sevadal. In 1971,

Mahesh Chander Mehta began publishing an English news weekly, *Presager*. In this weekly newspaper he exposed many scams, revealing corruption fearlessly wherever it existed. He even bought his own prinitnng press to cut down on expenses for newspaper printing and earned money by taking on outside printing jobs.

After acquiring a degree in law in 1974, Mahesh opened his own office in Jammu. In this office there were three other fellow-lawyers, who were honest and respectable citizens, practicing law. Mahesh kept busy in many other social activities. In this connection he used to devote his time between 4 o'clock and 8 o'clock daily in the evening to meeting and discussing problems of the people and offering them legal assistance.

Mahesh had a significant experience in his life. Once the famous journalist, Khushwant Singh wrote in his editorial for the *Illustrated Weekly of India* that in India, all the lawyers were more interested in earning their fees than wth seeing justice done. Mahesh got enraged on reading this criticism, as he particularly objected to Khushwant Singh's allegation of brandishing "all lawyers" as mercenary. He filed a defamation case against the journalist. In those days, Khushwant Singh was in a very strong position as he was a close friend of the then Prime Minister. At that time of Emergency, things could have gone against him as it was hardly the finest hour for the rule of law. Mahesh continued with his case undeterred. Ultimately Khushwant Singh had to appear in court, where he was granted bail. He had to print a pubic apology in his weekly. Thus Mahesh scored a victory in Jammu.

At the behest of some friends, Mehta helped to organise labourers working in shops, factories and other commercial areas in Jammu. They worked as daily wage earners near burning furnaces during the summer, at very low wages. A number of youth came to his office to ask him to head a youth organisation. Mehta reluctantly agreed but stipulated that he was a believer in *ahimsa* — non-violent agitation. With this group he began by launching

a low-key *dharna*, sit-in demonstation. Gradually Mehta's ideological foundations were becoming stronger. He joined the Hindustani Andolan in Jammu & Kashmir.

In 1983, Mahesh married a social worker and freelance writer, Radha. He and his wife decided to close down their newspaper office in Jammu and shift to Delhi. A year later in June 1984, their only child Tarini was born.

On reaching Delhi, Mahesh began taking up legal cases in the Supreme Court. On this effort of his, he was ridiculed by his fellow-lawyers. To come to Delhi and start practicing directly in the Supreme Court was simply unheard of but Mahesh stuck to his decision and continued to work.

A particular case related to Mahesh's involvement with the environment is significant. Once Mahesh attended a public meeting held in memory of the famous parliamentarian, Piloo Mody. At the meeting, he met a person making an allegation against him, saying that law merely meant earning money; no good work was being done. At this Mahesh wanted to know from the man the reason for his allegation. The man replied that the Taj Mahal was getting affected by pollution but the government was not doing anything about it. The man's allegation shocked Mahesh and he took up the case very seriously. It involved a long process of investigation and litigation.

So, very carefully Mahesh collected all the information on the situation and read the literature after having to search it out. With a strong investigative methodology, he grew interested in the Taj. Then, taking along his wife Radha with him, he met the environmental scientist, Prof. T. Shivaji Rao. All three of them then reached Agra to see the Taj Mahal personally. He had never before seen the monument. Mahesh noticed not only the astounding beauty of the Taj Mahal but also its destruction. Pollution had started not only yellowing of the surface of the beautiful marble,

but also rendering it hollow. On noticing this, he silently made up his mind to do something about it.

In 1984, a fully-prepared Mahesh filed his petition under Article 32 in the Supreme Court. In his appeal, which included statements on Taj Mahal, other historical monuments in its vicinity and the people living around the site, he stated that the life of the "living monument" itself was under serious threat as well as the life and health of the people living near it. He said that the petroleum refinery and other industrial units near the Taj Mahal were posing a grave danger to it, other historical monuments in the vicinity and the people living around it. He quoted from the Constitution which protects the right to life of every citizen and provision of a healthy environment. Earlier too, Mahesh had won a case regarding pollution of River Ganges on the basis of a similar argument.

This case of 'marble cancer' on Taj Mahal continued for long but ultimately in 1992, the Supreme Court gave its vedict in favour of Mahesh's appeal. The government had to carry out many changes. Industrial units were shifted; a separate hospital was set up to handle cases affected by enivironmental pollution in the refinery; provision was made for 50 beds in the hospital and a bypass was constructed. Further the to-and-fro road was taken far away and use of coal was banned in the vicinity. All the brick kilns were removed from an area of 20 kms around the site. This was a victory for Mahesh in favour of the Taj and the environment. Following this, he filed petitions in many cases pertaining to problems of environmetal pollution and established his awareness and conscious efforts in environment-related problems.

In 1985, nealy forty children returning from school were affected by a foul smell emitting from a drain in west Delhi. It was due to the discharge of chemical effluents by the Shriram Foods and Fertiliser Company. Mahesh, on behalf of these children, filed public welfare litigation in court, but the Registrar of the

Supreme Court refused to accept it. His argument was that the issue was not so important and serious to be taken up in the Supreme Court. He even advised Mahesh to work on his personal cases instead of wasting time on public welfare cases. This depressed Mahesh quite a bit.

Next, on 4 December 1985, an accident took place due to gas leakage at the Union Carbide factory in Bhopal. Thousands of people lost their lives. It created an outrage in the entire country. At this, Mahesh immediately got the papers of his earlier petition against the Sriram Company recovered and filed a petition again. The Supreme Court paid prompt attention to it. Mahesh's report was prepared so laboriously and systematically that the Supreme Court had no objection in accepting it. And so the Shriram Foods and Fertiltilser Company had to pay compensation. What is more, today whenever cases related to pollution arise, the 'Mehta doctrine' never fails to find mention.

This very year, Mahesh raised the issue of pollution of the River Ganges.

In this region many industrial units, including leather, were releasing their poisonous waste and chemical effluents. In Haridwar, it was even seen that if one threw a lighted match stick into the water, the water caught fire because inflammable material was reported to be floating on the surface of River Ganges. This river, flowing for 2,500 kms, was affected and even the people living nearby had to brave the influence of pollution.

Two years after Mahesh's efforts, in 1987, the government enforced closure of 21 leather-tanning units situated on the banks of River Ganges. Morevoer, the demand for compensation by the industrialists was turned down. Mahesh says, "I am not opposed to development. All I say is that public health and welfare shoud not be destroyed in the name of development."

Mahesh Chander is continuing with his struggle for protection

of the environment. His field of activity now takes him to Tamil Nadu, Andhra Pradesh, Orissa and the rest of the country. His only dream is to open an *ashram*/legal institution dedicated to both environmentally sound living and using the law as an instrument for environmental protection. He believes that to fight legally in favour of the people is a pious act.

JOCKIN ARPUTHAM

Awarded for Peace and International Understanding (2000)

It is a commonplace phenomenon of our times that millions of Asians pass their entire life in city slums. In these makeshift neighbourhoods, life goes on without being provided the most basic of facilities and living under the constant fear of eviction. Jockin took birth on 15 September 1946 as the eighth child of S. Arthupam of Tami Nadu at Arudayapuram of Kolar Goldfields. Jockin's parents believed in Catholic reilgion. A major portion of Jockin's life was spent in improving the life of slum-dwellers of Bombay by fighting for their rights and finding solutions to their problems. Encouraged by his Gandhian thoughts, Jockin brought out remarkable changes in the lives of slum-dwellers. He was awarded the Magsaysay Award of 2000 for extending his lessons of community building in India and South-east Asia and helping the urban poor of these parts of Asia to improve their lives by learning from one another.

In Bombay alone, some seven million people live in the slums. Jockin Arputham knew this world intimately for he was born and brought up in this environment. As founder and leader of India's National Slum Dwellers Federation, Arputham made it his lilfelong mission to alter this world for the better.

Jockin Arputham was not to the manor born, but neither was he born to extreme poverty as his work among the slums may suggest. His father served as a foreman in the Kolar Goldfields, which were owned and managed by the British. It was one of the largest private goldmines in India. Jockin's father was appointed president of the Panchayat. This post was highly esteemed at that time. He had contacts with the Chief Minister Kamaraj and as a result came to be interested in politics.

Jockin studied in a Kolar Goldfields school run by Indian Catholic priests, who used English as their medium of instruction. His parents wanted Jockin and his brothers to enter the seminary, but priesthood held no attraction for him. Jockin family was very well-off and Jockin was escorted to school by two orderlies walking on either side of him. Though the school was nearby, the orderlies carrying his bag, water bottle, etc. were symbols of the eminence of Jockin's father. Over the years, however, Jochin's father took to drinking and by the time Jockin reached Class VII, the family had lost all its land. Food became scarce at the Arputham home. The dwindling fortune drove a wedge between Jockin's parents and Jockin lost all interest in school. One day, he came home wearing only one worn-out shoe; he had thrown the other one away in a gesture of protest over his family's worsening poverty. It was the last time that Jockin wore shoes. Anger began to build up in his mind against his father.

While staying with the family, Jockin did remain religious but his belief in Catholic religion did not run deep. One day, in such a situation, Jockin announced that he did not want to remain a part of the family. He was barely sixteen. He took out ten rupees

from a jar he found in the house, put them in his pocket and got on to a train. He travelled to Bangalore without a ticket.

In Bangalore, Jockin's maternal uncle had a house. On reaching his house, Jockin did some minor jobs and learned carpentry in an inexpensive school. He had cousins on his mother's side who were doing well as carpenters; one of them offered to take him in as an apprentice. It was his first real job. Soon he began to feel that in comparison to other workers, he was being paid less salary. So Jockin first left his uncle's home and later left his job also. For a few days, he did some minor jobs and after staying in Bangalore for two years, he reached Bombay in 1963.

During the 1960s and 1970s, Bombay as the commercial centre of India drew hordes of migrants, mostly poor farmers or landless rural folk from other parts of the state as well as the country. Jockin set up his lodging in Mankhurd Colony which was an illegal slum area. Here he, along with many others, did carpentry and other small jobs. These workers gradually evolved into a community and from it emerged an informal school where hundreds of slum childen learned from their adult 'teachers'. These children used to earn money by singing and playing songs on old and empty Dalda cans and tambourine.

Here he set up a school-like shelter for illilterate children of the slums and began to teach them himself. From among them, some other persons came forward to teach and in this way, Jockin became a part of the life of the slum dwellers. He had seen poverty and was now seeing it again in its worse form. In Bombay, Jockin covered his nakedness while walking with "my hands pulling down my shirt, because the back of my pants didn't exist. There were two big holes. Even now sometimes, unconsciously, I walk pulling down my shirt," admitted Jockin much later.

Mankhurd Janata Colony was a neglecgted and dirty slum. Nobody was interested in keeping the area clean. There was no facility and neither did the people ever think about it. One of

the first steps that Jockin took was to do something about a garbage dump in the neighbourhood that had been ignored by the civic authorities. Marching to the local administration office, he and the children dumped a bag each of rubbish in front of the Bombay Municipal Corporation (BMC). Next day, the BMC staff came to catch hold of Jockin. Jockin told them firmly, "We keep the colony clean ourselves but BMC should come to collect the refuse." At his insistence, the BMC had no alternative but to give in to his demand.

Now Jockin desired to do something for this colony. In 1969, he constituted the Mumbai Slum Dwellers Federation. Its objective was clear from the very beginning: no evictions, no demolitions. If an eviction was inevitable, the Federation demanded that the people at least had the right to ask for a dialogue with the authorities. Arputham refused to register his Federation with the government, arguing, "Why do you want registration? To beg for money? To give an account to somebody? Only people who know how to read and write can run [the organisation]? But we are not educated, that's why we are talking."

In 1973, Jockin got married at the age of tweny-seven. His married life came only second to his public responsibilities. His wife, Rita, despite her unhappiness, gave him full support. She had also seen a time when she had to sell her saris for Jockin's work. Jockin too had to mortgage his typewriter during that lean period. Despite all such adversity he never fell victim to greed. He rejected the facility of a house, the proposal to enter the political field and never wavered or compromised. He weakened only once when prior to the Bombay problem, he attempted to commit suicide in Bangalore but failed.

In 1974, the Mumbai Slum Dwellers Association developed into the National Slum Dwellers Federation (NSDF). A significant turn came in this movement in the mid-1970s, when the Janata Colony was scheduled to be demolished to make way for the Atomic

Energy Commission. The NSDF responded by barricading roads, organising mass demonstrations, securing stay orders and fighting the eviction order all the way to the Supreme Court. The situation took a serious turn when Prime Minister Indira Gandhi took a personal interest in the demolition case. In 1975, Jockin personally went to New Delhi to demand an audience with her. She made him and his followers wait for twenty-nine days. Arputham went on a hunger strike. His twenty-four person delegation slowly dwindled to four as their resources became scarce.

After a long struggle, he won the sympathies of many parliamentarians and opposition parties. But Indira Gandhi gave the green signal for the demolition. At this, Jockin distributed leaflets printed in red letters to voice his objection. He even met the Chairman of the Atomic Energy Commission, who told him, "Even God will not be able to stop it tomorrow." At half past four the following morning, Arputham handed over the Court's order for a stay of eviction to the Chairman. But Jockin lost his fight as he had to leave when the police was called in. Jockin was imprisoned. It was even rumoured that he may be killed. On top of this, the British Broadcasting Corporation (BBC) announced to the world that Jockin, leader of Janata Colony, had been placed in police custody along with his followers and was about to be killed. Arputham Jockin thought it advisable to flee from the country for some time. In 1976, he left for the Philippines.

In the Philippines, Jockin took training in rehabilitation of slum dwellers at the Tondo Foreshore Area in Manila. He even contacted the Philippines Ecumenical Council for Community Organisation in Cebu city and after understanding their working style, returned to India in 1978. In the Philippines he had learnt that a policy of confrontation should not be adopted. Dialogue, he realised, was the key.

In the 1980s, Jockin's programme for improvement of slums became more widespread and NSDF entered into partnership with

organisations like the Society for the Promotion of Area Resources Centre (SPARC) and Mahila Milan. Around 1984, many other NGOs joined the NSDF, which reposed deep faith in Jockin.

In 1994, Jockin started his work in Poona, where in front of Rajendranagar Colony the danger of a similar sort of demolition loomed large as seen in Bombay. Almost half of Poona's 2.7 million population at that time lived in slums that were constantly under threat with demolition by the city's Municipal Corporation. Jockin led a long struggle but demolition had begun. The Municipal Commissioner advised the slum dwellers to look for alternative sites. So they took loans and got down to constructing their own houses.

During this period, many improvements were introduced in the slum areas due to Jockin's efforts, though not to the desired extent. Nevertheless, Jockin has been able to attract public attention both within the country and abroad. He has also been able to arouse the desire to work which is a significant development. It is said that the pavement may still be home for Jockin Arputham but today it is so by choice; no longer by a cruel twist of fate.

ARUNA ROY

Awarded for Public Service (2000)

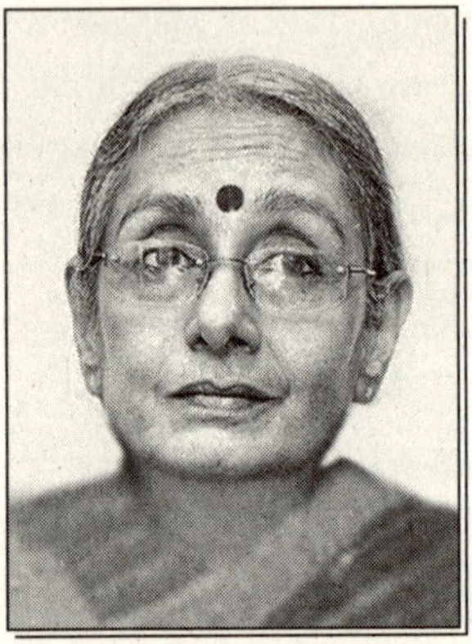

The most powerful weapon discovered to fight injustice and corruption is information. Aruna understood the might of the pen and launched a struggle against injustice and corruption. She discovered that the poverty-ridden and illiterate public of the country was the worst victim of injustice and exploitation. Therefore she founded the Mazdoor-Kisan Shakti Sangathan (MKSS) and launched her movement. The aim of the organisation has been to create awareness among the labour class and farmers of villages and organise them into a group so that they can work as a front to voice their demands. Aruna Roy was awarded the Magsaysay Award for the year 2000 for empowering Indian villagers to claim what is rightfully theirs by upholding and exercising their right to information.

Corruption is prevalent everywhere and more so in high places. But are the low places free from it? No; far from it. How much

of the development funds earmarked for the rural poor every year actually reaches the poor? Aruna Roy realised the weakness of the system as a junior officer in the Indian Administrative Service and decided to do something about it.

Aruna Roy was born on 26 May 1946 in Madras. Like a hardworking and intelligent student, she began to work in the Indian Administrative Service in 1968 after clearing the examination. As a newly appointed officer, Aruna was exposed to her country's diverse, poverty-stricken villages. She learned that she could not easily penetrate it, or change its ways, as an elite official. After seven years of service, she resigned. In 1974, she moved to Rajasthan.

Aruna began to work for a voluntary organisation, the Social Work and Research Centre (SWRC), at Tilonia in Rajasthan. The organisation, engaged in village-level development projects on health, education, gender and livelihood, had been established by Aruna's husband, Sanjit Bunker Roy. Her experience here convinced her that the poor people must be the agents of their own economic and social improvement and that political action is fundamental to their success. Aruna Roy worked with this organisation till 1983 after which she separated from her husband.

From here, Aruna reached the village named Devdungri in Rajasthan in 1987. She was accompanied by some of her fellow activists, like Shankar Singh and Nikhil Dey. With their help, Aruna established the Mazdoor-Kisan Shakti Sangathan (MKSS) in 1990. This organisation was started as an NGO which began working for labourers and farmers of the village. Its headquarters was in the village of Devdungri. Their group accepted no external funds and spurned the trappings of prosperous NGOs. Living as the poor lived and eating as the poor ate, Roy and her companions began assisting the villagers to assert themselves against the local power structure.

Meantime the rape of Bhanwari Devi in Rajasthan shocked

Aruna. It was the year 1992. Aruna Roy constituted a public forum of twenty bright women and old men. A massive demonstration was staged in Jaipur where Aruna coined the slogan, "*Izzat gayi kiski? Balatkariyonki!*" (Whose respect was lost? Of the rapists!). This slogan had been prepared by Aruna's female companions. It was an unusual demonstration against sexual harassment and it culminated in the historic Vishakha judgement given by the Supreme Court over this issue.

Her organisation MKSS set many new trends. Apart from rejecting financial assistance from external agencies, Aruna guarded itself against the hold of powerful and established NGOs and local powerful groups. Using traditional forms of protest, such as hunger strikes and sit-ins, the MKSS-led villagers insisted that the local people hired for state projects be paid the legal minimum wages. They forced a land-grabbing feudal lord to return the encroached-upon land to the legal but poor owners.

Most provocatively, the MKSS held open-air public hearings at which official records of state development projects were exposed to the scrutiny of the intended beneficiaries. Shocking revelations came to the forefront -- toilets, schools and health clinics were recorded as paid for but were never constructed; improvements in wells, irrigation canals and roads were shown but remained noticeably unimproved; famine and drought-relief measures were never rendered; and wages were shown as paid to workers who had been dead for years.

Aruna Roy explained to the people that the right to information is the first and foremost need – bills, vouchers, employment rolls included. Leaders of the MKSS campaigned for public hearings. It became a campaign for transparency in government. "Our money, our records," chanted the villagers. There was a unanimous demand for transparency in the working of the government and the right of the public to inspect the records pertaining to their salary and work.

Despite the campaign by Aruna Roy, the officials were loath to open their records. This prompted Aruna and MKSS to launch a series of rallies culminating in a fifty-three-day protest in Jaipur, the capital of Rajasthan. The state government was forced to reveal the records of the Vikas Fund to the public. This movement soon gained nationwide support. Intellectuals, political activists and media joined Aruna Roy and ultimately the law for the right to information was passed in Rajasthan and three other states.

Aruna Roy enlightened the labourers and farmers by creating awareness among them on the law. If an issue or a situation disturbs her, she says, "I am not comfortable until I do something about it."

Keeping the Magsaysay Award money aside in a trust, Aruna Roy is using it for organising democratic struggles in favour of the working class.

RAJENDRA SINGH

Awarded for Community Leadership (2001)

Even in the best of times, it is dry and arid in the Alwar district of Rajasthan. Yet not so long ago streams and rivers in Alwar's forest-covered foothills watered its villages and farms, creating a generous if fragile human habitat. People lived prudently within this habitat, capturing rain-water in small earthen reservoirs called johads *and revering the forest, from which they took sparingly. In the 20th century, miners and loggers decimated forests and damaged the watershed. Its streams and rivers dried up followed by its farms. Dangerous floods now accompanied the monsoon rains. Most of the menfolk moved to cities in search of jobs as the region faced a serious problem of water. Rajendra Singh, by understanding this problematic situation at the basic level decided to solve the issue. He established the Tarun Bharat Sangh in which young volunteers revived the traditional* johads *that had gone dry and solved the problem of water to a considerable extent. Rajendra Singh was awarded the Magsaysay Award of 2001 for leading Rajasthani villagers to the steps taken by their*

ancestors in rehabilitation of their degraded habitat and bringing its dormant rivers back to life.

In the 1930s, the Alwar region was witness to abuse of forest tracts through large-scale deforestation. In the 1940s, the ruler of the state decreed that the forest be given to charcoal contractors, leading to the death of hundreds of trees and the loss of livelihood for the local inhabitants. The merger of the state with the Indian Union in 1947 did not see much improvement in the situation. What Rajendra Singh saw when he first arrived in 1985 were "naked hills all around." And this set him working.

Rajendra Singh was born on 6 August 1959 at Daula village of Bagpat district, Uttar Pradesh. His father was a farmer who mangaged 60 acres of land that was planted with sugarcane, rice and wheat along with other crops. Rajendra spent his childhood here, playing in the fields with animals.

As Rajendra was the first grandson, he basked in the affection of his grandfather and his uncle who lived together as members of an extended family. After passing high school, Rajendra had his first taste of actual social work. A worker named Ramesh Sharma from the Gandhi Peace Foundation, came to live with his family and invited Rajendra to get involved in improving the life of the villagers. Rajendra would notice Ramesh go around the village, cleaning it, settling conflicts and establishing a library or a place for debate. He also showed the people how to help themselves.

Rajendra acquired a degree in Ayurveda from the Bharatiya Rishikul Ayurvedic Mahavidyalaya in Barot. After graduating from this private college in Ayurvedic medicine and surgery, he decided to work for the welfare of the people by practicing this traditional system of medicine in his village. Along with this, enthused by Jayaprakash Narayan's call, he was drawn to politics and so formed the Chhatra Yuva Sangharsh Vahini (Student-Youth Struggle Battalion). Rajendra chose to do postgraduation in Hindi in a college

affiliated to Allahabad University at Barot.

Having completed his studies and lacking a better option, Rajendra joined government service in 1980 at Jaipur. He was appointed as the National Service Volunteeer for education. Here he was given charge of a project for adult education in Dausa district of Rajasthan. Meanwhile, his father got him married and his wife Meena joined him at Jaipur village.

Rajendra did not like his job. Moreover, he was gradually getting troubled by the situation in Rajasthan which was suffering from a perennial water problem.

In 1981, when he had been married only for one-and-a-half years, he left his job. His wife Meena left their home to visit her parents and did not return. With his wife gone, Rajendra sold off all the household items that she had accumulated for Rs 28,000. And thus he jumped into his field of activity. He resolved to find a solution to the water problem in Rajasthan. Keeping aside Rs 8,000 in the bank, he took the remaining sum for this work.

Four other friends joined him and they were Narendra, Satendra, Kedar and Hanuman. All five of them founded an organisation named Tarun Bharat Sangh which was given the form of an NGO. Actually this organisation had been founded by Jaipur University in 1978 but it had gone defunct. Rajendra Singh revived and adopted the project. This way Tarun Bharat Sangh (TBS) became his project.

To begin the TBS movement on 2 October 1985, Rajendra Singh and his friends reached Kishori village of Alwar district which was twenty hours away from Thanagazi. Now Rajendra did not know what to do next and how to start. He found out a map and identified an area of 55 kms at the base of Aravalli mountain range. All five of them boarded a bus and reached there. Because these five bearded strangers appeared in the village not long after the broadcast that terrorists had entered the village, they

were surrounded by the villagers who mistook them for terrorists.

Now began the dual struggle for TBS. Firstly, they had to win over the confidence of the villagers who were unable to understand the reason for giving up their jobs to live among them and secondly, they had yet to decide what they wanted to do to find a solution to the water problem. Whatever they wanted to learn, they hoped to learn from these illiterate-looking villagers! In this, the feeling of pride in some of his friends served as a deterrence. But Rajendra Singh was convinced that he had to find some way or other to overcome the problem.

After discussing with the villagers and obtaining information on the situation in other areas, a solution to their problem seemed to be in sight. They decided to revive the old wells and *johads*. These *johads* had been lying dry for ages and these five persons from the TBS had no idea about how to dig the wells. On seeing their dilemma, a landlord named Seth Badri Prasad came to their rescue. He offered them the use of his house and donated Rs 500 to them.

The five of them went around the village wondering why the land was so dry and barren! Why in spite of 600 mm of rain there was no groundwater? A 60-year old man named Mangu Lal Patel advised them, "If you are interested in helping the village, build a *johad*. A *johad* is a semi-circular pond for collecting the run-off from the tiny streams and rivulets of a much wider area. No engineer is required to dig it; all that is needed is will power." Making Mangu Lal Patel their companion, they selected Gopalpura village for starting their work. This village had been without groundwater for five years.

As a first step, arrangement had to be made for storing the rain-water in the earth. To prevent the rain-water from spreading and flowing out, an enclosure was built to store the water. Rajendra organised the youth of the village to rebuild a neglected check-

dam's earthen wall and scrape the silt off the *johad*, moving the rich topsoil to the fields. When the monsoon came, the pond began to fill with water, which then seeped into the earth and recharged the water-table. Fresh water now filled the wells that had been dry for years. The villagers were elated to see this.

Twenty kms away, a village named Bhaonta-Kolyala, noticed that Gopalpura village now had water in its wells all the year round. On 6 March 1987, a site for digging the first *johad* was selected here. A Gram Sabha was organised to seek assistance from the entire village. For this, responsibilities were fixed on each household. They were even explained how to repair and clean a *johad* after its construction so that it continued to remain useful. The work began and through their own labour the villagers saw that water filled in the *johad*. Along with this work, sites for other *johads* were identified.

Enthusiasm ran high in the village after the success of the first *johad*. Taking the cue from them, people in the other villages along the River Arvari began to repair and build their own *johads*. Little did the villagers realise that by coming together to rejuvenate their environment, they were also reviving the river. TBS began to dream of this river flowing again. Work started on building a big dam in 1990. A high dam of 244 metres in length and 7 metres high was constructed so that the rain-water would not flow away before penetrating deep into the earth. In 1995, with hard labour at every step and saving of every drop of water, River Arvari began to flow again. As a result, other streams also got revived to begin flowing again in this region.

The effect of this revolution reached the other distant villages. When a stream began to flow from the Jabbar Lake in Hamirpur village, boats too began to ply on it while fish are also reared.

Rajendra proudly said, "The government has finally conceded that people's cooperation alone will make such work sustainable

and permanent." When Rajendra Singh and his companions look at the progress they have achieved, they cannot help but remember the unmemorable day when they first reached Kishori village, the villagers nabbed them, mistaking them for terrorists. However, their persistence to do something for the villagers of Rajasthan has not gone in vain. It is as a result of their conviction that villages in Rajasthan have begun to lead a new life, free from drought.

SANDEEP PANDEY

Awarded for Communiy Leadership (2002)

The youngest Magsaysay awardee of the country, Sandeep Pandey was so disturbed to see the underprivileged and poor people living on the edge of poverty that he resolved to work for their welfare. He founded an organisation named Asha Parivar to fulfil his resolution and through this he began to work for welfare of the Dalits and the minorities of the country. He worked enthusiastically with this organisation and started a programme for which he launched a countrywide awareness campaign. For setting the empowering example of his commitment to the transformation of India's marignalised poor, Sandeep Pandey was awarded the Magsaysay Award of 2002.

Mahatma Gandhi, after studying abroad, returned to India. He left a comfortable career as lawyer and devoted himself to politics. As though following his example, Sandeep Pandey returned home from America to forego a comfortable career and apply himself to the country's social problems.

Sandeep Pandey was born on 22 July 1965 in a middle-class Brahmin family of Ballia in Uttar Pradesh. After completing his schooling from a local school, he joined Benaras Hindu University. He left for Berkeley in USA to obtain a doctorate degree in Mechanical Engineering from California University. Here he met Deepak Gupta and V.J.P. Srivastavoy, who, despite staying abroad, were gravaely concerned for India and wanted to support education of poor children. The three of them joined hands and constituted Asha (Hope) Parivar to support education by tapping the resources of the Indians abroad. In one year they raised 10,000 US dollars to disburse for programmes in India.

In 1991, armed with a Ph. D. degree from California University, Sandeep returned to India and took up a job as Lecturer at IIT, Kanpur. Through the Asha Parivar, Pandey's main aim was to remove corruption in the political establishment, increase its efficiency and force it to become more responsible. He wanted the impoverished, low-caste families and Dalits of the land to obtain information regarding their rights. He desired to build up their self-confidence so that they could be prepared to fight for their rights on their own.

The society had declared them outcasts and they were leading a life of misery. Collecting together the local *swayamsevaks* (volunteers) of Reoti and Bhainsaha, Sandeep made arrangements for providing education to the deprived. He made a beginning in this direction by setting up schools that instilled self-confidence and self-reliance within them. He wanted to establish a society based on justice and equality. It was his belief that Asha Parivar was the first *ashram* (hermitage) of the *swayamsevaks* working for the impoverished poor. Members of Asha undertake the teaching themselves and do not draw any salary; instead, they support themselves by making candles and greeting cards from handmade paper which they sell. Students too learn useful art and crafts. The older youths participate in

community development by working as volunteers and health aides. They are part of what Pandey calls "the first grassroots volunteer base of Asha in India."

After Reoti and Bhainsaha villages of Ballia, Sandeep began the expansion of Asha Parivar among the Dalits of Lalpur village in Hardoi. Here he taught the students to live and study among traditional artisans and engage in bee-keeping, vegetable gardening and cottage industries. They follow a special Asha curriculum where they sing songs and read stories to the local inhabitants to highlight the school's philosophy.

The Asha Parivar fulfils, besides *ashram* education and awareness about rights, other responsibilities like providing simple health facilities. Through this medium, the organisation also publicises anti-Dalit crimes and abuses, such as bribes-taking by local officals. Sandeep even includes programmes to create awareness about cleanliness and sanitation as a part of the normal learning process. Arvind Pandey tells them the importance of its implementation and has started a campaign on inculcating cleanliness as a habit.

Asha Parivar is introducing new technologies and livelihood projects. "The objective of the organisation is to link the grassroots endeavours to the the larger task of shaping the socio-economic political future of the country," says Pandey. Asha Parivar now claims thirty-six North American chapters and has disbursed more than one million dollars for programmes aimed at bringing about socio-economic change in India through education.

Sandeep Pandey denounces any policy that creates a schism between the different communities and calls for an end to "the politics of revenge" that drives the country to communal violence. Volunteers of the Asha Parivar are engaged in trying to convice the Dalits that their place is in the mainstream, not in the periphery.

Sandeep's awareness is not confined merely to Dalits or the

poor but refers to other fields too. After the Pokhran nuclear test, Sandeep launched a 1,000-metre long *padyatra* (walk) against such a test, beginning from the site of the Pokhran blast to Somnath, the centre of Buddhist enlightenment. This march was called the Global Peace March against the nuclear test and in welfare of the public. Sandeep Pandey said, "The voice of peace has to be louder."

Sandeep Pandey's involvement includes betterment of relations between India and Pakistan too. Like Pokhran, Sandeep lauched a *padyatra* campaign with the aim of improving Indo-Pakistan relations. This march took place from Delhi to Multan and was considered a significant beginning at the fundamental level in Indo-Pakistan relations.

Sandeep leads the National Alliance of People's Movements (NAPM), the largest network of grassroots people's movements in India. NAPM includes groups like the Fish Workers Forum led by Father Tom Kochery, who organised protests against specific religious groups. NAPM includes representatives of organisations like the Christian Institute for the Study of Religion and Society, Madurai and attracts activists like Mercy Mathew, a nun working under the name of Dayabai among the Gond tribe. These organisations are involved in work centred on Adivasis and other minorities.

Sandeep Pandey's fearless and determined personality can be gauged from the following incident. When he was awarded the Magsaysay Award, he announced boldly, "The biggest terrorist nation in the whole world is America," during the acceptance speech. When challenged by the Filipino media, he returned the prize money.

Sandeep wears *khadi* clothes and is a Gandhian. He says, "I believe in the Gandhian thinking that once the path is chalked out, the means will follow." Criticism does not deter him and he does not miss any opportunity to criticise any wrong step taken

by the government. He even served as an advisor to the Indian Government's Central Advisory Board for Education (CABE).

Sandeep Pandey continues to work for his movement while living with his wife Arundhati and their two children in Lucknow.

JAMES MICHAEL LYNGDOH

Awarded for Public Service (2003)

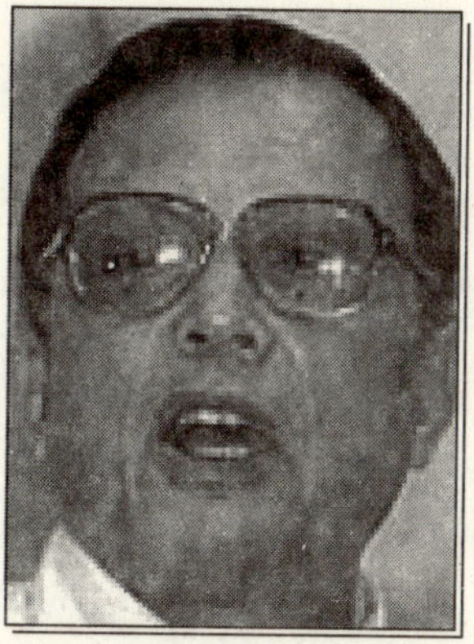

Despite diversities and different castes in India, the roots of democracy run deep and the credit for this goes to the Constitution and the bureaucracy which implements this difficult task with discretion. James Michael Lyngdoh too fulfilled the most taxing responsibility of conducting impartial and just elections as the Chief Election Commissioner of the country. In his own way he exercised his strong determination and control to organise elections in the strife-torn Jammu & Kashmir state. This way he maintained the confidence of the people despite the many diversities and different religions. Lyngdoh was awarded the Magsaysay Award of 2003 for his convincing validation of free and fair elections as the foundation and best hope for secular democracy in strife-torn times.

India is a country of nearly 700 million voters and it is no mean job to organise free and fair elections in all the states of the country.

This immense and elaborate responsibility rested on the shoulders of James Michael Lyngdoh in 2002.

James Michael Lyngdoh was born on 8 February 1939 in India's north-eastern state of Meghalaya. Of Khasi tribal origin, Lyngdoh hails from the extreme north-eastern corner of India. Imbibing moral rectitude from his father, a District Judge, Lyngdoh completed his education in Delhi and entered the elite Indian Administrative Service when he was barely twenty-two. He quickly became known for probity and toughness and for favouring the underdog against the politicians and the local rich.

Initially itself Lyngdoh annoyed the local landlords with his reform programmes because of which he was transferred before he could complete even one year. But there was no change in his attitude or his determination to continue to work as before.

He had confrontations with his officers, his staff, local leaders and eminent persons of the society with whom he was firm but cordial. Lyngdoh had to suffer mental tension but it did not affect his promotions. His rise in service continued. And rise he did, eventually as Secretary, Coordination and Public Grievances, Cabinet Secretariat, Government of India. In 1997, the President named him as one of the three Election Commissioners of India. By 2001, he became the Chief Election Commissioner.

Now he was faced with the grave responsibility of holding elections in the strife-torn Jammu & Kashmir state, in 2001. On the one hand, the Central Government was locked in a potentially explosive standoff with Pakistan and on the other, feelings of antagonism among the Kashmiri secessionists towards the country ran high. Further, there was the danger of an attack from across the border and the need to persuade the local population to participate in full strength in the elections. Both the conditions were not easy to bring about.

In such a situation, Lyngdoh used his own discretion. He knew that cancellation of elections would amount to escapism.

No problem could be solved this way. Many people were doubtful of the elections being held fairly and successfully. Lyngdoh, however, proved them wrong. Pushing ahead despite all the criticism, he updated and verified the election rolls, introduced voter identity cards and added a thousand new voting sites. He recruited non-paritsan poll officers for every polling station. After warning the army to stand clear but ready, he heightened the election security by mobilising the local police and paramilitary forces from outside the state. He urged the pople "to vote fearlessly". Nearly 44 per cent people voted. Even Lyngdoh's critics had to acknowledge that polling had been fair. In this way, the "ballot won in front of the bullet". It became an example that despite such a difficult task in Jammu & Kashmir, the sanctity of democracy was maintained.

Lyngdoh faced his second big challenge in Gujarat. In the last days of February, as a result of the murder of fifty-eight Hindu pilgrims, the Hindus in Gujarat went on a killing spree and in retaliation, killed thousands of Muslims. Property and wealth of the Muslims was looted and their houses burnt. In this tense situation, many Muslims escaped to far away places in search of safety. At this time, the BJP government was in power. It dissolved the State Assembly and started clamouring for early elections. Lyngdoh used his authority to say 'no'. Citing the large number of displaced persons and the pervasive atmosphere of fear in Gujarat, he postponed the elections. A little later he began making arrangements for organising free and impartial elections. In the process, instead of making the local administrators and police to work in the elections, Lyngdoh transferred them and arranged for security forces on a large scale from outside the state. He imposed strict restrictions on public movement to curb violence during the election campaign and established new voters' booths at places where Muslim refugees lived. In the month of December, with strict security measures in place, elections were held in Gujarat. Nearly 61 per cent voting took place. Critics of Lyngdoh were

forced to admit that the arrangements for the elections were beyond criticism and the elections were held in an impartial manner.

Due to his image as a strong administrator and his personal contacts with the people, Lyngdoh carved a special niche for himself in the government department and ministries. He was strict but he could never be accused of favouritism or atuocratic behaviour. To facilitate his work, Lyngdoh adopted two new rules and these he followed explicitly. The first rule was to keep himself away from publicity. He did not allow either his friends or detractors from hanging around him. This way he saved himself from giving speeches which would have brought him unduly into limelight and in the news. Similarly, he followed the other rule of keeping himself away from political leaders, parliamentarians and ministers. Despite a disciplined conduct he maintained such a distance that the people could not reach him. Thus Lyngdoh did not allow any pressure from politicians, flatterers, critics or media to come in his path. He reaped the benefits of his policy later in life.

James Michael Lyngdoh, as has been said of him, had been a silent crusader blessed with an inner strength, so long as he was in power. He now leads a retired and peaceful life.

SHANTHA SINHA

Awarded for Community Leadership (2003)

Child labour due to poverty is prevalent in cities and villages. Children from poor families, who do join the school for some time, are forced to drop out inevitably to take up some employment to become their parents' support. Shantha Sinha did the work of removing child labour from the state of Andhra Pradesh. She proved wrong the belief of the people that the poor cannot survive without the earnings of their children. This way, as Secretary of her organisation, Mamidipudi Venkatarangaiya Foundation (MVF), she imposed restrictions on child labour and made arrangements for their education. She fulfilled this responsibility with full conviction despite every objection. She was awarded the Magsaysay Award of 2003 for guiding the people of Andhra Pradesh to end the scourge of child labour and send their children to school.

Many people held the belief that if the poor families of Andhra Pradesh did not send their children to serve as child labour in

households, or to harvest cotton seeds and flowers, or to tend to goats of their neighbours, their families would be still poorer. Shantha Sinha, however, thought otherwise.

She was born on 7 January 1950 at Nellore in Andhra Pradesh. She completed her postgraduation in Political Science in 1972 from Osmania University. She obtained her doctorate in 1976 from Jawaharlal Nehru University in Delhi.

Shantha Sinha used to remain disturbed since the very beginning at the plight of young children working and often thought of doing something in this direction. As head of an extension progamme at the University of Hyderabad in 1987, she organised a three-month long camp to prepare children rescued from bonded labor to attend school. This experience of hers proved very encouraging.

In 1991, she placed her views before her family and founded an organisation in the name of her grandfather.This organisation was called Mamidipudi Venkatarangaiya Foundation (MVF). The objective of this organisation was to put an end to child labour in the whole of Andhra Pradesh and start the tradition of sending every child to school.

Shantha began her project in poverty-ridden villages of Ranga Reddi district. Members of the organisation encouraged the local people to identify out-of-school and bonded children and urged their parents and employers to release them. Shantha Sinha also invited the employers of child labour to attend her training programme. This way the MVF put in sincere effort for a long time so that the thinking of the people could be changed to encourage them to make their children study in schools. They then organised training camps to prepare the children to attend schools. They found supporters of their cause among the youth, teachers and local officials. With assistance from local and international donors, they expanded their activities.

By 1999, the MVF was active in 500 villages. But the parents

were not easily convinced. They questioned how any working member of a family could be sent to school and deprived of his services. For these families their childen, who were engaged in labour, were like full-fledged earning members. Words like 'child' or 'childhood' held no meaning for them. They felt that education, school, all these were meant for the rich families. The members of MVF tried to convince them that freedom from poverty could be obtained through education. This situation was difficult both for MVF and Shantha but the parents had to be won over, come what may.

Slowly and gradually temporary schools were started by Shantha for training the children. She organised transition camps to prepare the children to attend school. Soon the transition camps grew into full-fledged residential 'bridge schools'. Using familiar songs, riddles and newpapers, volunteer teachers developed the children's basic skills and introduced them to the pleasures of reading. They then exposed them to a formal curriculum to prepare them to enter a pubic school. Either through the 'bridge schools' or direct enrolment, some 250,000 former child workers could acquire education.

Shantha Sinha held the belief that as the children had emerged from non-formal schools they must attend regular schools rather than part-time schools. Part-time schools do not generate the enthusiasm among this category of children that is needed. That is why she tried to train the children to learn what would be required in regular schools so that they could be treated as equals.

In the process, Shantha Sinha was able to make arrangement in the year 2000 for education of about two-and-a-half lakh children who were earlier working as child labourers. Through her movement she focused not only on child labour but made arrangemens in her scheme for providing adult education too. Shantha Sinha had been working with many such schemes of the Indian Government. In the 1980s, she was attached to the Political Science Department

of Hyderabad University and her attention was fully focused on attracting willing adult workers who were engaged in employment in the direction.

Shantha Sinha also served as Director of Shramik Vidyapeeth. On joining this institute, she came to learn that not a single agency was working with full devotion in this direction. So she accepted the challenge and took up the cause of freeing the country from the evils of child labour and bonded labour.

Nearly 30,000 volunteers and countless youth clubs, village education committees, teachers' groups and other organisations are carrying the spirit developed by Shantha to take the work ever further. Through this ripple effect, the Foundation is creating a social climate hostile not only to child labour, but also to child marriage and other such practices that deny children the right to lead a normal life. Today, the MVF's 'bridge schools' and programmes cover more than 4,300 villages.

Shantha Sinha was awarded the Albert Shanker International Award in 1999 by Education International, USA. The same year she was honoured with the Padmashri. At present she heads the National Commission for Protection of Child Rights. This Commission was set up in March 2007. Professor Sinha is its first chairman.

LAXMINARAYAN RAMDAS

Awarded for Peace and International Understanding (2004)

India's Partition following the country's Independence had created an environment of distrust and anger between the people of India and the newly created nation of Pakistan. The Kashmir issue has led to a further deterioration in relations, showing no signs of improvement. Disturbances and mutual distrust have continued to increase. Dismemberment of East Pakistan from West Pakistan has heightened the tension. That is why the bitter relations between India and Pakistan have affected the peace process. Laxminarayan Ramdas of India alongwith Abdur Rehman of Pakistan constituted a 'Pakistan-India People's Forum for Peace and Democracy' to work towards peace and democracy. Both Laxminarayan Das and Abdur Rehman were given the joint Magsaysay Award of 2004 for their combined efforts to reach across a hostile border to nurture a citizen-based consensus for peace between Pakistan and India and for trying to demilitarise and denuclearise South Asia at the international level.

The armed conflict between India and Pakistan has endured for more than sixty years, bringing with it four outright wars and continued upheavals. Its flashpoint is Kashmir, claimed by both sides though its roots lie in the communal violence of Partition in 1947. However, Laxminarayan Das of India and Ibn Abdur Rehman of Pakistan believe that there is hope for the two countries to become good neighbours and friends.

Laxminarayan Das was born in 1933 in Bombay. At the time of India's Partition, he happened to be in Delhi. On completing his education, he was selected by the Indian Armed Forces Academy, Dehradun and was sent for training to the Royal Naval College, Dartmouth, England. After completing his course, Laxminarayan joined Indian Navy as a commissioned officer.

While working in the Navy, Laxminarayan remained head of the Naval Academy at Cochin, Kerala but during his entire tenure of service, the Indo-Pakistan war of 1971 remained at the top of his mind. In this war he had to face Pakistan's warrior tanks which came rushing to bomb East Pakistan (now called Bangladesh). One of his major accomplishments was the reconnaissance and interdiction of the enemey vessels and bombing of East Pakistan during the Indo-Pakistan war. East Pakistan emerged as an independent nation with a new name—Bangladesh. In 1990, Laxminarayan Ramdas rose to the post of the Chief of Naval Staff.

After retiring from the Navy, Laxminarayan Ramdas focussed his time and energy to bring about peace between India and its neighbour Pakistan and in September 1994, Laxminarayan Ramdas joined twenty-four like-minded Indians and Pakistanis in Lahore to open a public dialogue for reconciliation and peace. This led to formation of the 'Pakistan-India People's Forum for Peace and Democracy'. Laxminarayan Ramdas was appointed Deputy Director of the Indian branch and Abdur Rehman became the founder Director from Pakistan in the organisation.

The prime weapon of this Forum was communication, as it considers communication vital for knocking down the wall of discord. Since 1995 the Forum had begun working in this direction.

Thousands of Pakistanis and Indians have raised their voice, demanding lessening of troops on the border. Their aim is to take the issue to both the people and the governments of both sides and make them decrease the strength of armed forces on either side of the border. For Rehman, the Forum's peace initiative grew naturally from his work as one of Pakistan's leading human rights advocates and as a long-time Director of Pakistan's Human Rights Commission. He says that both India and Pakistan should reject their "pathological obsession with the politics of hostility." He adds, "I entered the armed services as a hawk and exited as a dove." His military career has made him conscious of the limitations of military solutions to political problems. He says that the nuclear test in May 1998 was "one of the greatest turning points in my life." With this, Laxminarayan Ramdas and his wife Lalita got busy in a campaign against nuclear weapons. He issued a warning to both India and Pakistan for dependence on such an armament, asking them to emerge from the vice-like grip of nuclear weapons.

Laxminarayan also recalls with great emotions the scene when he was only fourteen-years old. This was just before the birth of Pakistan. His family in Delhi had hidden some Muslims in their house to protect them. Laxminarayan said that on one side there was the refugee Muslim family and on the other, the fear of the enraged crowd which was searching for Muslims in every corner of the country to kill them. Such scenes were bound to sow seeds of hostility among them.

Both Laxminarayan and Rehman connect the problem of peace in the subcontinent with dangerous ideologies that associate religion with nationalism and patriotism, to militarism and other anti-democratic forces. Both of them are continuing with their

efforts to bring about peace in the subcontinent. Through the efforts of Laxminarayan and Rehman, both India and Pakistan began to hold summit meets turn by turn in their respective countries so that the people's base in the Forum would increase. For ten years this process continued. Similar other forums which held the same objective were constituted.

Due to contacts with this Forum, environment, human rights, trade unions, rights of women and other fields of activity too have begun to be discussed at business academies and other professions. Clearly the strength of the Forum has begun to increase. Many programmes for face-to-face discussions and exchange of views between lawyers, diplomats, soldiers, artists and students have been organised. Its objective is to make both the nations raise issues at the politicial level while being alive to the aim of removing differences between them.

Rehman has said in reference to war and peace, "I believe the people are a little ahead of the governments." Laxminarayan is convinced that the understanding of the people of the two countries has been better than that of their governments. Hence, he feels convinced that his movement would prove successful.

V. SHANTA

Awarded for Public Service (2005)

Cancer cases are on the rise in India, particularly among men who usually suffer from cancer of throat, leg and stomach due to use of tobacco. Among women, cancer of neck and breast is very common. Dr V. Shanta did a lot of work at the Chennai Cancer Institute and conducted treatment and experiments under her own supervision in this neglected field. Dr V. Shanta was awarded the Magsaysay Award of 2005 for her leadership of Chennai's Cancer Institute in making it a centre of excellence and compassion for the study and treatment of cancer in India.

In an era when specialised medical care in India has become highly commercialised, Dr V. Shanta, a passionate advocate of cancer prevention, strives to ensure a cure for everybody from cancer. She says, "When the sick approach the gates of the Cancer Institute, weak in body and spirit, and full of fear, there is only one response: you have to become a part of them."

Dr Vishwanathan Shanta was born on 11 March 1927 at Mylapore in Madras. She was born into a family of academics and scientists, most eminent among them were scientist Chandrashekhar who was her maternal uncle and famous scientist and Nobel Prize winner C.V. Raman, who was her maternal grandfather's brother. As such precedents of successful people were present in front of her eyes since childhood.

V. Shanta's school education began at National Girls High School which has now become Sivaswami Higher Secondary School. Shanta wanted to be a doctor since childhood. She graduated from Madras Medical College in 1949 and completed her postgraduation followed by MD in 1955.

Meanwhile in 1954, Dr Muthulakshmi Reddy had established the Cancer Institute at Madras. Shanta successfully cleared the examination of the Public Service Commission and got herself registered at the Women and Children's Hospital. But when she realised the problems of the Cancer Institute, she spurned a lucrative post at the Women and Children's Hospital, annoying a number of persons in the process. She chose to join the Cancer Institute on 13 April 1955 and has remained here ever since. This step is ample proof of Shanta's concern for cancer patients and her humane feelings.

When the Institute was started, it was a very small building with limited treatment facilities. Apart from her, there was only one other doctor whose name was Krishnamurty. For the first three years, V. Shanta worked as a non-salaried doctor but later she started getting Rs 200 per month along with residential quarters in the hospital premises.

V. Shanta laid the foundation for the first cancer clinic in the country. She conducted a survey of cancer cases in the country and on the basis of it chalked out a programme for diagnosing cancer cases in their early stage in the villages.

At the Cancer Institute, V. Shanta revealed her obsession with her subject. She continued experiementing and when she discovered

the presence of a cacinogenic element in tobacco, she decided to control cancer among men. She opened a clinic to help men to give up tobacco.

V. Shanta's interest lay equally in research and experimentation. After a very serious study, she took the step of experimenting with a 'combination therapy'. In India, such an experiment had not been conduced earlier. It was a step taken after a great deal of consideration as its result was not known beforehand. V. Shanta's experiment proved successful and the 'combination therapy' produced miraculous results. With this success, a way was found for controlling and treating cancer of the mouth.

With this success V. Shanta's effors at experimenting further did not stop. Her efforts only gathered momentum. She coducted research on cancer of throat, neck and breast and made the blood disease leukaemia in children her next target. She got the results of her experiments published in the *International Medical Journal* and discussed it all over the world. In 1975, she converted the Cancer Institute into the first Regional Cancer Research and Treatment Centre in the country. As Director from 1980 onwards, Shanta strove to make the Institute a world-class research centre with institutional partners from Euorpe, North America and Japan with the state-of-the-art laboratory and imaging equipment. She worked tirelessly to raise donations, grants and government subsidies. She also trained hundreds of village-health nurses to screen rural women for cervical abnormalities.

V. Shanta did not rest on her laurels. In 1984, she expanded the Institute to make it a postgraduate college. Here V. Shanta began to train cancer specialists. Thousands of doctors acquired training in this college and are now working all over the world in their fight against cancer.

Through sustained efforts she opened India's first hereditary cancer clinic in 2000.

Beginning as a 12-bed hospital with two doctors -- V. Shanta and Dr S. Krishnamurthi, the founding-Director and Reddy's son,

the hospital developed to become a more than 428-bed hospital. Here Dr Muttulakshmi College of Oncological Sciences was set up in which all facilities for finer investigations and diagnosis are provided. In India, where the health facilities have become highly commercialised, the Institute is not only providing treatment at a concession of 60 per cent to the poverty-ridden patients but also taking care to provide their travelling expenses too.

A voluntary unit has been started to provide emotional support to cancer patients. By talking to them, the patient's psychological strength and self-confidence are built up as the patient stands on the precipice of death with certainty. As such, along with treatment psychological support is of great importance.

Dr Shanta has her own philosophy of life. She has the determination to work all twenty-four hours for the welfare of her patients. She wonders how people can spend liberally for donation to temples and on pilgrimages but when it comes to donating money to the Insitutue, they think twice. In Shanta's eyes, the treatment of human beings is the highest form of God-worship. She admits, "We seem to have got enough money to construct pilgrim shelters and temples in almost every street of the city." Perhaps reflecting on her own life, she says, "Learn to accept that you are good and that from you a lot of good can happen."

For V. Shanta service to mankind is the greatest award. In the campus of the Institute many patients can be found who consider their life a gift from Dr Shanta. She says that when a weak, dejected and a frightened patient knocks on the doors of her organisation, then her first step is to become a partner in his or her pain.

V. Shanta has been honoured with the Padma Shri in 2006. She is a member of the Advisory Committee of the World Health Organisation.

ARVIND KEJRIWAL

Awarded for Emergent Leadership (2006)

A weak civil and administrative system, where redtapism and corruption flourish, leaves an adverse impact on the minds of the public. This situation has to be changed in every developing country. Arvind Kejriwal deeply undertsood the need for such change and established an organisation whose objective was to free mankind from such ills. This organisation was named 'Parivartan' (Change). As an income-tax officer, he had seen the many powers that tax officials held over private citizens and how easily these powers could be misused. To achieve success in his work, he felt the need for keeping the citizens informed at what stage their work had reached and what was to be the next step. In the process he exerted pressure on the government to make the proceedings more transparent in government departments. Arvind Kejriwal was awarded the Magsaysay Award of 2006 for activating India's right-to-information movement at the grassroots and empowering New Delhi's poor citizens to fight corruption by holding the government answerable to the people.

Corruption among the high and mighty may create headlines, but for ordinary citizens it is the ubiquity of everyday corruption that weighs heaviest. And how demoralising this can be was realised by Arvind Kejriwal, founder of the welfare organisation called 'Parivartan' (Change).

Arvind Kejriwal was born in 1968 in Hissar town of Haryana. He was a science student and brilliant in his studies since the very beginning. With his capability, he passed Mechanical Engneering from IIT, Kharagpur in 1989. He then began to prepare for the IAS examination. He was successful in getting selected for the Indian Revenue Service in 1992. He was appointed in the office of the Income-tax Commissioner in Delhi.

While working here, Arvind Kejriwal saw much which he did not like. Corruption was rampant and tax-payers, not being familiar with the management, had to run from pillar to post. Ultimately, in desperation they would take assistance from unscrupulous persons on shocking terms and conditions. Arvind found this situation troublesome and began to ponder over this. Gradually he thought of some ways to root out corruption and introduced some changes in the system. The initial outcome was good.

Encouraged at his success, Arvind Kejriwal began to think of taking his activities forward. In January 2000, he took a sabbatical from work and started a movement for citizens in Delhi to lay the foundation for his organisation called 'Parivartan'. Through this organisation, a transparent and answerable administrative arrangement was demanded by the citizens of Delhi. Slowly Arvind Kejriwal's movement began to gain momentum. Since it was emotionally a social movement, he began to get support from the public.

Arvind Kejriwal's resolution to force the government to pursue a transparent and answerable policy was not that easy. For this, he had to struggle a lot while working in the department. When

his demand was not heard initially, he submitted a plea for public welfare in the Income-tax Department for introducing transparency through a five-point programme. He went on a *dharna* in front of lthe Chief Commissioner's office. He threatened to present his next objection in the presence of the press and the media. It had some impact as the chief of the department agreed to implement the five-point programme.

On leaving the Income-tax Department, Arvind went on a *dharna* with his other colleagues of 'Parivartan' in front of the Electricity Department. He also advised the future consumers not to offer any bribe for getting their work done. 'Parivartan' got grievances cleared with the Electricity Department on behalf of individual citizens. Many persons benefited from the organisation's 'Don't pay bribes!' campaign. As many as 2,500 cases were solved at the Electricity Department while saving many people from being fleeced.

While establishing 'Parivartan', Arvind Kejriwal began to support Aruna Roy's movement for Right to Information Act. This slowly turned into a quiet social revolution. With the support of the people and through the concerted efforts of 'Parivartan', the Right to Information Act was passed in Delhi in 2001. Under this Act, every citizen possesses the right to inspect government documents. Kejriwal put the law to use in Sundernagari, a slum in Delhi where 'Parivartan' was working among the poor. Firstly, the organisation obtained official reports on all recent public projects in the area. Next, it led residents in a 'social audit' of sixty-eight projects, stirring the community to action through neighbourhood meetings and *nukkad natak* (street plays). Then in a large public hearing, the residents presented their findings and exposed misapproriations in sixty-four of the projects with embezzlement to the tune of seven million rupees. Today in Sundernagari, local committees monitor public projects block by block and no project is begun until details of the contract are made public.

Arvind Kejriwal got married in 1995 to Sunita. Sunita, also from his batch, has been working with him since the beginning. With their two children, she gives equal support to Arvind in his campaigns.

Encouraged by his success in Sundernagari, Arvind Kejriwal spearheaded a campaign for enforcement of the Act at the national level and it was passed in 2005. The right to information holds as much importance in the lives of the poor as it does for the general public and professionals. Yet many Indians remain passive spectators. Arvind Kejriwal uses the Right to Information Act to equip individual citizens with the power to question their government. They have the right to see the related documents in their cases to check on the comment given by the concerned authority. Arvind Kejriwal wants to create awareness through the Act among the people so that they could vote for the right government after using their own discretion.

In one area, over 90 per cent of the grain ration had been skimmed off by shopkeepers in colllusion with certain food department officials. When 'Parivartan' investigated this, one of its team members was savagely attacked. In protest, more than 5,000 residents of the community held a month-long 'rations fast'. This and a mass rally drew public attention and foot-dragging officials had to move fast to clean up the system.

'Parivartan' is engaged in work with just ten members. Arvind Kejriwal undertakes large issues only once in a while. In 2005, it took up a successful campaign challenging a water-privatisation plan for New Delhi. He has no plans to expand. He prefers to coordinate 'Parivartan's' efforts with other like-minded NGOs across India.

It may be a long way to go before the RTI becomes a powerful tool for the common citizen, but Arvind has shown that there is a way possible.

In the year 2004, Arvind Kejriwal was awarded the Ashoka

Fellow Civil Engagement Award. In 2005, the IIT at Kanpur honoured him with the Satyendra Dube Memorial Award. This award is given for helping to bring about transparency in the government. The CNN-IBN electronic media honoured him with the 'Indian of the Year' title.

PALAGUMMI SAINATH

Awarded for Journalism, Literature and Creative Communication Arts (2007)

The prime role of journalism is to present a true and correct picture of the country. In the early twentieth century, the press was at the heart of India's freedom struggle. During those formative years, Palagummi Sainath, as a sharp and experienced journalist, felt that journalism contributed to "the liberation of the human being". In contrast, modern journalism is failing in its duty and is working only for big industrialists and high government officials. With this realisation, Sainath took up this challenge of journalism on his shoulders. He discovered that the acute misery of India's poorest districts was not caused by drought, as the government made it out to be. It was rooted in India's continuing structural inequalities — poverty, illiteracy and caste discrimination — and exacerbated by recent economic reforms favouring foreign investment and privatisation. Sainath through his understanding highlighed their condition as the first step and forced the state administration to take action on this.

P. Sainath was awarded the Magsaysay Award of 2007 for his passionate commitment as a journalist to restore the rural poor to India's consciousness, moving the nation to action.

With growth and technological development, the economy surges and matters that call for urgent attention of the public and the government are ignored in favour of film starlets and beauty queens, the stock market and India's IT boom.

Believing that "journalism is for the people, not for shareholders", P. Sainath doggedly covered the lives of the less fortunate.

Palagummi Sainath, as he was named at birth, was born in a distinguished family of Andhra Pradesh in 1957. The late President of India, V.V. Giri was his parental grandfather. Sainath had his education at Loyola College in Madras. He reached Delhi to study at Jawaharlal Nehru University from where he obtained his postgraduate degree in history. He was an active memberof the JNU Executive Council.

In 1980, Sainath began his career as a journalist by joining the United News of India. While working here, he was awarded the highest award given to any journalist. From here he shifted to *Blitz* magazine, an important weekly published from Bombay with a circulation of 6,00,000. He took charge of the department for foreign affairs and became Deputy Editor of the magazine. P. Sainath remained with the *Blitz* for ten years.

On leaving *Blitz*, Sainath became a Visiting Faculty for a special media course in Sofia Polytechnic, where young female journalists are provided training in the country. Sainath is still connected with this institute.

In his race to acquire experience, Sainath confronted many such situations which made an immense contribution in moulding him. He toured and studied ten drought-stricken states of the country. He learnt so much about them that he was deeply disturbed and remarked, "That's when I learned that conventional journalism

is above all about the service of power. You always give the last word to authority. I got a couple of prizes which I didn't pick up because I was ashamed."

About journalists he once said very ironically, "There are two types of journalists – those who are genuine journalists and those who are merely stenographers who take dictation from their bosses."

Khwaja Ahmed Abbas had said about him in 1984, "Sainath is incorrigible, irreverent, indefatigable and, at times, infuriating. To this I shall add one more word: incorruptible. Friends, I introduce you to the most irreverent voice in Indian journalism. I bring to you the man who will go through life being the boy who said, 'The Emperor has no clothes...' I don't know another journalist who cuts to the heart of a matter past all hypocrisy and camouflage so clearly and with such humour. I do not know another journalist who can make compassion so compelling."

In 1991, Manmohan Singh took up the responsibility of introducing economic reforms on behalf of the International Monetary Fund. This step constituted a watershed in India's economic history and in Sainath's journalistic career. He felt that the media's attention was moving from 'news' to 'entertainment': consumerism and lifestyle of the urban elite getting prominence in newpapers which rarely carried news on the reality of poverty in India. "I felt that if the Indian press was covering the top 5 per cent, I should cover the bottom 5 per cent," said Sainath.

In 1993, he submitted an application for a fellowship in *The Times of India.* During the interview, he gave a description of his plan for development of rural India. At this, the editor who was interviewing him, asked, "If I say my readers have no interest at all in this subject, then?"

Sainath argued by asking, "When did you last come face-to-face with your readers that you can make such a claim on their behalf?"

P. Sainath got the fellowship and he chose the work of studying

the ten poorest and backward districts of five states. Sainath had to travel extensively and he did it all bravely. He covered one lakh kilometres all over the country, completing his journey in sixteen different modes of transport, including 5,000 kms on foot. In this period, when, in the field of journalism, *The Times of India* was being called a newspaper which had shifted from Page one news to Page three news, then P. Sainath's eighty-four page report on the rural situation was published for eighteen months under the fellowship. Sainath's journalism disturbed many organisations and units ideologically. He found an opportunity to learn much from this. *The Times of India* set an example for other newspapers in reporting issues related to poverty and uplift of villagers.

These articles were subsequently reprinted in his book, *Everybody Loves a Good Drought*. For two years, this book remained the topmost book in India. It was called Penguin's "all-time bestseller". Even today non-government organisations consider this book as an important handbook for its free style of direct reporting on social and economic cleavages in society. Whatever royalty was given for this book to Sainath, he donated to a fund constituted for awarding young rural journalists.

As a reporter Sainath proved the power of the press repeatedly. In one state after another, the bureaucracy and politicians acted upon his stories preferring this to confrontation or denial. Today, more than any other journalist in India, he has been responsible for the attention drawn to cases of farmers' suicides in the country. He has been instrumental in establishment of the Agriculture Commission in Andhra Pardesh to suggest ways of improving agriculture in the state.

A documentary film titled *A Tribe of His Own* was made by Joe Moulin in Canada, keeping Sainath's works as the theme. It received an award at a film festival. The Director of the film invited Sainath to join him in receiving the award because the film was an "award about inspiration".

P. Sainath has received nearly thirty national and international recognitions. He was awarded many honorary degrees by various national and international organisations.

P. Sainath is currently working as Editor on rural issues for the newspaper, *The Hindu.*

PRAKASH AMTE AND MANDAKINI AMTE

Awarded for Community Leadership (2008)

On getting freedom from British rule, India took the path of development and achieved considerable growth. But the Adivasis, who have been living in forests and barren regions for centuries, have seen neither growth nor change even after sixty years of Independence. They, as citizens of India, do not receive even recognition as Indians, leave alone any facilities. Adivasis of Madia Gond caste too are victims of this tragedy. They inhabit a dense forested region of 150 kms located in eastern Maharashtra bordering Andhra Pradesh and Chhattisgarh. Carrying forward the tradition of his father Baba Amte, Prakash Amte along with his wife, who like him is a qualified doctor, are concentrating their work on this Adivasi area. After building his Anandvan Ashram in the area, he settled down to start treatment of the Adivasis in addition to imparting information. In 1973, Baba Amte along with Albert Schweitzer had begun a people's

community cenre for health and educational needs of the Adivasis. Prakash Amte and his wife too joined this centre. They were awarded the Magsaysay Award jointly of the year 2008 for their community service and for enhancing the capacity of the Madia Gonds to adapt positively in today's India through healing and teaching and other compassionate interventions.

Hidden amidst the dazzling human mosaic of India are millions of tribal people. The Madia Gonds are one of the tribes of Maharashtra who live in remote highland and forests, away from civilisation. Like his father Baba Amte, Prakash Amte and his wife decided to work for the welfare of these tribals.

Prakash Amte was born on 26 December 1948 and brought up at Anandvan, founded by his father Murlidhar Devidas Amte who was a renowned Gandhian humanitarian.

Prakash took his medical postgraduation degree from G.M.C. of Nagpur and began practicing medicine in the city. In 1974, he received a message from his father to join him in the region inhabited by Madia Gond Adivasis and start working for them. At his call, Prakash and his newly married wife Mandakini abandoned their urban practice in Nagpur and in a leap of faith, moved to remote Hemalkasa. Mandakini too was a postgraduate doctor and had been employed in a government hospital at that time.

The Amte couple settled down in a doorless hut, without telephone, electricity or privacy. They practiced medicine beside the roadside and warmed themselves by burning firewood at night. The Madia Gonds, shy and suspicious of outsiders, spurned their help initially. Prakash and Mandakini befriended them, learned their language and patiently won their trust. The miraculous cure of an epileptic and a man close to death from cerebral malaria turned the tide. "Once a patient gets cured, he comes back and brings

four new patients," says Prakash. They set up their own dispensary under a tree and tried to help the tribals.

Thus Prakash and Mandakini created a place for themselves among the Adivasis. In 1975, with financial assistance from Switzerland, a small hospital was set up at Hemalkasa where the best medical facilities were provided. At this hospital it became possible for Prakash and Mandakini to conduct minor operations also. They treated through modern techniques the patients suffering from malaria, tuberculosis, diarrhoea/dysentery as well as those burned by fire or bitten by snakes and scorpions.They carried out hospital work as far as possible outside the hospital, under a tree, to suit the lifestyle of the Adivasis and without charging any money from them.

This project is called Lok Biradari Prakalp, a project for the development of tribal people in the forest of Gadchirolli district. The project seeks to provide health and educational services to tribals in this district. Hemalkasa lies in a tribal belt and the couple provides health care to about 40,000 tribals who inhabit this area.

Prakash and Mandakini realised that due to illiteracy the tribals had been often exploited at the hands of corrupt officials of the Forest Department and other greedy persons. The Amte couple began to give them advice regarding their rights besides explaining their problems to forest officials on their behalf. Through concerted effort, Prakash got corrupt forest officials transferred from there and established a school in Hemalkasa in 1976.

The Adivasis were initially hesitant to send their children to school but with time, the school grew. Along with reading and writing, the Adivasis were imparted education related to their employment. Prakash and Mandakini's own children too began to study in the same school.

The Hemalkasa School provides information to the Adivasis on farming, horticulture and irrigation and makes them understand

the importance of preservation of the forest. Under forest preservation, the Adivasis are also taught to protect wild animals. The Amte couple has also founded an orphanage for taking care of wild animals so that the lives of the cattle can be protected and the balance of Nature maintained. Surprisingly enough, since the inception of this orphanage, the Adivasis have reduced their habit of eating meat. They have begun to subsist on grains and other farm produce.

The involvement of Prakash Amte in his work can be gauged from the fact that he was so engrossed in running around and moving to and fro that he came to know of his becoming a father much later. He was so filled with happiness at this development that he recorded this as an unforgettable incident in his life. This also shows how he could get so lost in work as to forget himself even.

The simple lifestyle and conduct of the Amte couple among the Madia Gond Adivasis has converted them also into tribals. The two of them are now an integral part of the tribals' life. Their style of dressing has become similar to that of the Adivasis. Prakash wears ony a singlet and white shorts as he goes about his work, so as not to identify himself with 'well-dressed' outsiders. Wherever possible, the couple incorporates tribal cures in their medical practice as they have acquired knowledge and training in treatment with herbs and plants.

At the school established by the Amte couple, the Adivasi children have begun to acquire training in dance and music, while remaining in touch with Adivasi culture. The school has grown to 700 students and is comprehensive. Among its graduates are the Madia Gonds' first doctors, lawyers and teachers as well as officials and police. Prakash says with happiness, "More than 90 per cent of the students have come back to serve in the community, including my sons. Maybe it's the way we have led our lives."

On receiving the Magsaysay Award, Prakash said, "I accept the award on behalf of my entire team dedicated to the cause of social welfare and upliftment." He, however, has one regret – "Baba would have been happy if I had got the award in his lifetime."

DEEP JOSHI

Awarded for Community Leadership (2009)

Despite all round progress and development in different spheres of life, poverty remains persistent and widespread in India as almost forty-two percent of its population still lives below the global poverty line. Besides governmental agencies, a number of non-governmental agencies are working to alleviate this poverty. It is in this context that Deep Joshi emerged to fight against the poverty through a non-profit aorganisation PRADAN (Professional Assistance for Development Action). This organisation recruits university educated youth from campuses across the country and grooms them to work at grassroot levels. Living and working with the poorest communities of the country, PRADAN empowers village groups with technical, project implementation and networking skills so as to enable them for income generation, and also trains villagers as technical professionals for building and sustaining collective livelihood projects. Deep Joshi was awarded the Ramon Magsaysay Award in 2009 for his vision and leadership in bringing professionalism to the NGO movement in India.

Little did the people who are not in the development sector know about Deep Joshi before he was awarded the prestigious Magsaysay Award. However, he is a well known name in the development sector who has revolutionised the rural development work in India.

Deep Joshi was born in 1947 at Puriyag, a remote backward village in Pithoragarh district of Uttarakhand in a well-to-do family of farmers and was one of the seven children of Harikrishan Joshi. Joshi received his early education at the local village primary school after which he moved to Allahabad from where he obtained his engineering degree from Motilal Nehru National Institute of Technology. After the completion of his engineering education, Deep Joshi took up a teaching job. Meanwhile he got a national scholarship from the Indian government and went to USA to pursue his doctorate in engineering. After he was awarded the Ph.D. degree, he returned to India and started working with the System Research Institute in Pune which was trying to introduce management and systems in cooperation with the public sector or NGOs. In 1977, Deep went to Jamkhed in Ahmednagar, Gujarat to work on 'Comprehensive Rural Health Project', a project set up by a doctor couple Raj Arole and Merul Arole. It was his first experience of working in the development sector. Deep was deeply impressed with the Aroles and their work. He realised that if more people equipped with sophisticated training and knowledge and empathy decide to work in remote backward areas, India's rural society could be completely transformed.

Deep also worked with the Ford Foundation of India as a programme officer. At the Foundation he was sent to study a successful model of water users association near Chandigarh. To his surprise the model was defunct on the ground and he conveyed the same to his seniors. He was instructed to restart the functioning of the association. Being an expert in System Analysis, he succeeded in restarting the model of water users association. Such field experience in the area of development work

encouraged him to work whole-heartedly for community development and it was the germination of the seed of PRADAN.

Deep left his job at Ford Foundation in 1983 and completely devoted himself to the task of setting up PRADAN, alongwith his friend Vijay Mahajan. In the beginning it was a tough time for Deep as there was a shortage of funds and staff. Initially, PRADAN functioned as a third party, providing professionals, taking responsibility of pulling in youth from premier educational organisations like Indian Institute of Management (IIM) and Indian Institute of Technology (IIT) and sending them to work at village levels. Later PRADAN started its own direct community intervention programme and became successful within a short time.

PRADAN works to empower village groups with technical, project implementation and networking skills that increase the income generating capabilities of the villagers. Besides, it trains villagers as para-veterinarians, accountants and technicians who support their fellow villagers in building and sustaining collective livelihood projects. This organisation has a strong network of three hundred professionals and over a thousand graduates covering over 170,000 families in over three thousand villages of India's poorest states.

According to Joshi, poverty is a result of lack of capability and also because of historical exclusion. Over a period of time the way society has developed under various influences have excluded some people and included some people. So their ability to reintegrate themselves back to society takes time and it requires initiatives and earnestness to make them aware and restore confidence in them.

Today, Deep Joshi advises the Government of India on poverty alleviation strategies and is also a member of Working Group on Rainfed Areas for the Eleventh Five-Year Planning Commission of India.

❑❑❑

NILEEMA MISHRA

Awarded for Emergent Leadership (2011)

Dedicating one's entire life for a social cause is neither easy nor very common. So, if someone does that he/she must be an exceptional person. That is what we can call Nileema Mishra. At the age of 13, she resolved not to marry and work for the development and welfare of her village, Bahadarpur in Maharashtra. Her master's in clinical psychology was her first step towards her goal. Her organization BNGVN lends money to the poor through microfinancing and self-help groups. Her efforts have changed the lives of poor rural women who are now financially independent.

Nileema Mishra is not a rich philanthropist who does social work in her spare time. She is a middle class woman driven by her passion to serve the poor, especially women. Nileema was born in Bahadarpur, a village in Maharashtra. Social work is in her genes as she belongs to a family of social activists. She was only 13 years old when she decided not to marry and work for poor. Since then now 39-year-old

Nileema has been working tirelessly to achieve her aim of eradicating poverty.

Nileema did her master's in clinical psychology from Pune. She did not choose this subject to get a comfortable, well-paid city job, which she could easily get, but to gain knowledge and skills which would help her in her development work. For eight years she worked with Vigyan Ashram in Pune district.

When Nileema returned to her village and talked to the women about their problems, she realized that most of their problems were related to the lack of money. These problems could be solved with easy access to credit. With this aim in mind, Nileema and her friends formed Bhagini Nivedita Gramin Vigyan Niketan (BNGVN), or Sister Nivedita Rural Science Centre, named after an Anglo-Irish missionary who spent her life helping poor Indian women.The NGO took small but significant first steps. It formed a self-help group (SHG) of 14 women and taught them how to save money. Later many such SHGs were formed. Today the number of SHGs is 2,000 with 20,000 beneficiaries across Maharashtra.

These SHGs enabled the women to get micro credit and start home-based enterprises such as food products and export quality quilts. BNGVN trained the women in production, marketing, accounting and computers. These income-generating activities made these women financially strong.

BNGVN also helped the cotton farmers who were committing suicides due to failed crops. BGVGN formed a rotating fund which provided loans to farmers. It also built 300 private and communal toilets.

Nileema has infused confidence and optimism in the villagers that they can solve their problems without being dependent on anyone. Nileema says, "Our philosophy is not to beg but to create self-reliance". As the citation for the Magsaysay Award states, " In electing Nileema Mishra to receive the 2011 Ramon Magsaysay Award for Emergent Leadership, the board of trustees recognizes the

purpose driven zeal to live and work tirelessly with villagers in Maharashtra, India, organizing them to successfully address both their aspirations and their adversities through collective action and heightened confidence in their potential to improve their lives."

HARISH HANDE

Awarded for Emergent Leadership (2011)

Passion drives people more than money. Harish Hande is a perfect example of this. Harish, a US-trained Indian energy engineer, provides cost-effective solar energy to the poor. This is not a small achievement in India where half of the population does not have access to electricity. His efforts have not only improved the quality of life of the poor but also contributed towards reducing climate change.

Harish Hande, born in Banglore, did his doctorate in energy engineering from the University of Massachusetts. While studying in US, he visited Dominican Republic and realized that to provide solar energy to the poor in villages, it is necessary to use "small scale, stand-alone" installations. After returning to India he visited the villages to understand their situation.

Harish established Solar Electric Light Company (SELCO) in Banglore in 1995. The company's main aim was to provide cheap energy to the rural poor. It makes PV lighting systems, water heating

systems and cooking stoves. The company provides customised products as per customer needs. It also provides doorstep after-sales service. To help poor buy solar energy, SELCO helps them get finance from rural banks, cooperatives and even SHGs.

SELCO has sold more than 1, 15,000 solar home lighting systems in 15 years. It has 25 energy service centres in Karnataka and Gujarat. SELCO has proved that social ventures can be commercially viable besides promoting a sustainable energy model.

■■■